All Together –
Creative Prayer with Children

ALL TOGETHER –
Creative Prayer with Children

Ed Hone and Roisín Coll

VERITAS

First published 2009 by
Veritas Publications
7/8 Lower Abbey Street
Dublin 1, Ireland
Email publications@veritas.ie
Website www.veritas.ie

ISBN 978 1 84730 179 6

Designed and typeset by Barbara Croatto
Printed in the Republic of Ireland by ColourBooks Ltd., Dublin

Veritas books are printed on paper made from the wood pulp of managed forests. For every tree
felled, at least one tree is planted, thereby renewing natural resources.

About this book

Teachers in Catholic schools (and parishes) regularly look for resources for praying with children: for prayers, ready-made liturgies and, especially, for ideas. Often, this can be something that is rushed or last-minute: for example, there's an assembly coming up soon, or a classroom prayer session scheduled for the next morning, and something has to be produced at short notice. This book is not primarily about providing ready-made resources; it is, rather, something we believe to be much more useful. It is suggesting a way to work with children when putting together school assemblies and classroom worship, tapping into the children's creativity, enthusiasm and real-life concerns.

Although this book can be used to dip into at the last minute, this is not its purpose. Rather, it really will reward a closer reading and a familiarity with the principles that we suggest are vital for praying with children. All of the principles and the prayer ideas suggested are the result of real classroom experience, and the more familiar you are with them, the more creative prayer with children will become second nature. The expectation of producing classroom prayer sessions or school assemblies will not be borne by you, the teacher, alone: it will be shared with the children, who will be your chief resource.

Section One is the basis for the whole book and is essential for understanding its purpose and getting the most from it. Section Two contains insights, explanations and creative resources for different liturgical seasons and occasions, but also for encouraging personal prayer. Each chapter offers different approaches to creative prayer.

We have seen how creative classroom and assembly prayer can be of benefit to you, the teacher, to your children and to the wider school community: an enlivening and enriching experience for all.

Ed Hone and Roisín Coll

Contents

Acknowledgements

Special thanks are due to the following: the Department of Religious Education at the University of Glasgow; Hazelbank School in Glasgow for hosting our workshops on creative liturgy for children with additional support needs (ASN/SEN); Veritas Publications for permission to reproduce Chapter 1 which first appeared in *Exploring Religious Education: Catholic Religious Education in an Intercultural Europe* (Kieran and Hession, 2008); and Dr Patricia Kieran and Sr Pat Gribbin for their advice and encouragement. Finally, a special thanks to the children with whom we have worked over the years – your energy, creativity and faith inspired us to write this book.

Roisín and Ed

Foreword

One of the joys in my own personal life as a Bishop is visiting Catholic primary schools. Always evident are the openess and joy of the children, and it is wonderful to see their natural reaction to everything about them and, especially, the way they respond to love.

If our primary school children respond to the love of an adult, how much more must they respond to the love of God as they grow to realise the immensity of that infinite love and how that love was channeled in the love of Jesus Christ.

It is the primary responsibility of parents to direct the prayer life of a child – but that responsibility must be shared also by our primary school teachers as well as by our priests. That simply is what I believe this book entitled *All Together – Creative Prayer with Children* is all about!

The book does not give any ready-made answers. Rather, it helps parents, teachers and priests to grow and deepen in their own prayer life as they help children realise more of the wonder of their relationship with God and how to express that relationship through their thoughts and in their words. Helping a child grow in the light of the love of God is, quite simply, similar to watching a flower burst into full bloom in the light and heat of the sun. What a wonderful responsibility is ours!

I heartily commend this book as a wonderful resource which will make the responsibilites of a class teacher, as well as those of parents, priests and also visiting bishops, ever more fruitful and joyful in themselves.

With every blessing
† Keith Patrick Cardinal O'Brien
Archbishop of St Andrews and Edinburgh

Section One
Chapter 1
The Foundations of Creative Prayer with Children

Introduction

Classroom and assembly prayer play a vital role in the life of the Catholic school. Where children and teachers work together and recreate together, it is only appropriate that they pray together too. In a Catholic school context prayer is not viewed as a duty but as a natural expression of what it means to be Catholic Christians. The disciples said to Jesus, 'Lord, teach us how to pray' (Luke 11:1), and he readily taught them.

Preparing classroom prayer can be both challenging and immensely rewarding. As a teacher engaging in prayer with children you need: to believe in the value of what you are doing; time to plan and rehearse; lots of energy, enthusiasm and a good dose of imagination. The task, however, need not be daunting. The key is, as always, working *with* children, not *for* them. When you work in this way you engage the children so that the prayer becomes *their* prayer and *their* minds and hearts are raised to God. In this chapter we primarily address creative prayer with children in classroom and assembly situations. Whilst the context here is school, the same principles and practice apply in all environments where people work with children in prayer.

What is liturgy?

The word 'liturgy' comes from the Greek and literally means 'the work (*ergon*) of the people (*laios*)' – and liturgy is the bringing of the lives of the people to God. When people come to worship God *together* this is called liturgy. When we speak of liturgy in school, we are not talking about the official Liturgy of the Church (the Mass, the Divine Office, the celebration of the Sacraments); rather we mean praying together by using words, silence, signs and symbols. This kind of prayer is also referred to as 'para-liturgy'; that is, unofficial collective prayer. This chapter will focus on liturgy as classroom prayer and also on school and classroom assemblies.

Liturgy is about God, and liturgy is about us. We bring our lives to God when we worship, and the spiritual strength and inspiration we receive we take back into our lives. Our liturgy gives God praise and gives us life. This is true for adults and children alike. The school classroom, with its community and its routine, is a good place for liturgy. In our classroom prayer and assemblies we bring this community and routine to God. God blesses us, hears our prayer, and helps us with our daily work.

Liturgy and community

Liturgy is the prayer of a community and really belongs in community. It is something we do together, where we open ourselves to each other and to God. In liturgy we share our hopes and fears, we pray for ourselves, each other and our world and we thank God for everything God does for us. In classroom and assembly prayer, we usually pray, in the plural – 'God, hear *our* prayer', 'Lord, hear *us*' – rather than as individuals – 'God, hear *my* prayer', 'Lord, hear *me*'. God is at the heart of our community, so it is only right that we should pray, and when we pray we are helped to live our lives more fully. The Gospel tells us, 'Where two or three meet in my name, I am there among them' (Matthew 18:20). Our prayer together makes us more sensitive to each other's needs, more aware of our own need of God's help, more willing to face the problems of life, knowing that we are not alone. The community is with us and God is with us. If we think of the Mass, the first words we say match the first gesture we make: the Sign of the Cross. We are acknowledging that we are in God's presence. At the end of the Mass, however, the emphasis is different: 'The Mass is ended, go in peace' or 'Let us go in peace to love and serve the Lord'. The emphasis here is on going out into the world, carrying with us something of what we have received. In short, liturgy takes us from our encounter with God into our full engagement in life.

Where liturgy takes place and why it is important in the school prayer and liturgical celebrations are central to the life of a Catholic school, and it is recognised by the Magisterium of the Church that the Catholic teacher has a responsibility to help children engage with God. 'The teacher will assist students to open their hearts in confidence to Father, Son, and Holy Spirit through personal and liturgical prayer.'[1]

If there is adequate provision for prayer, it is during this time that God can communicate directly with children, and they have the opportunity to respond fully in adoration and praise, in thanksgiving and in petition. In order to maximise the impact of any prayer experience for children, time should be set aside that is neither rushed nor seen to be simply an add-on to the day.

'If we want to sustain a relationship with anyone, we must spend time with that person. We must try to find the **way** in which we can **best communicate** with each other. Likewise, with God, if we want to help children to relate to God, we need to help them to become aware that God is present in their lives. We also need to help them communicate with God: to be able to talk to God in prayer and to be able to listen to God speaking to them in the silence of their own heart.'[2]

Traditionally, prayers are said at the beginning and end of the school day, as well as before and after lunch. However, there are many other openings that provide children with liturgical and prayer experiences throughout the school week. In both the primary and secondary school, assemblies provide opportunities for children and students to participate in active and creative communication with God. The effectiveness of assemblies is inevitably reduced where the teacher or someone in senior management takes sole responsibility for writing the material and instructing the children in what to say and do. Using the *children* as the chief resource means that the materials for assemblies can be created by working together, sharing ideas and tapping into the children's own prayer experience and culture. Ultimately, children should have ownership of their prayer-time. They will then be sharing their own faith with their peers in a way that will be understood and sympathetically received.

Having ownership of the liturgy is vital for two reasons. First, if children are directly involved in the preparation of the prayer, then the opportunity for *catechesis* is present. The teacher can work with the children as they plan the prayer while directing, informing and explaining to them the relevance of their work. Catechesis can take place not only through the prayer itself but through its preparation. Second, ownership is important because it enhances the *experience* of worship. If the children have been involved in its planning and implementation, then their understanding of it, engagement with it, and response to it will be strengthened. When children present an assembly or engage in classroom liturgy they have ownership of what they do, they are more committed to the project, more energised, and consequently communicate more effectively. All who participate in the prayer will gain more from the experience.

What liturgy (and preparation for liturgy) can achieve

It is worth repeating that in classroom and assembly prayer, the *process* of producing liturgy is as important as the end result. There is a world of difference between the teacher giving the class a script for classroom prayer, and the children being encouraged to generate one for themselves. Pupil and teacher creativity is vital. However, the teacher must be a realist and should be aware of what classroom and assembly prayer can achieve. It is important to consider age and ability differentiation. For example, it is impractical to think that young children can engage in meditation for long periods of time or even compose elaborate prayers. Furthermore each prayer time should have a particular aim. For example, a liturgy on the theme of friendship could have the aim of encouraging the children to be kind to others as Jesus is kind to us.

Below are outlined some of the positive effects of creative prayer with children in the classroom:

- Classroom prayer can bring the class together, uniting teacher and children more closely.
- Prayer can help those who take part to reflect more deeply on life, giving them a new understanding of something which concerns them.
- Prayer can help children to give voice to their longings and hopes (and, of course, their fears and concerns).
- Prayer can instruct, painlessly catechising children whose knowledge of faith grows through engagement in liturgy.
- Prayer can motivate, giving a new determination to a class, so it might then wish to actually do something practical after having been inspired in prayer.
- Lest we forget, classroom prayer can entertain. It is not always solemn and worthy – God enjoys humour too!

Knowing what you want the prayer to achieve is vitally important. We all know the impracticality of engaging children in an action song, for example, and then trying to calm them down to do some serious work!

Classrooms are often such busy places that it should not be surprising to discover that silence can play an important part in classroom prayer (though it is harder to achieve in an assembly situation). Careful attention must therefore be paid to the effective *creation* of silence. Reflective music, simple chants (e.g. Taizé), a gently paced liturgy, all help in the creation of silence. Silence is shaped by what surrounds it, what comes before it and what follows it. The silence you create in the classroom may be solemn, joyful, expectant, grateful, sorrowful, even exuberant – depending on how it is created.

To whom do we pray?

Consciously or not, when we pray we have some kind of image or understanding of God in our mind. God might be the judge we have to appease, the friend with whom we can be ourselves, the parent who nurtures us and makes us feel safe (or of whom we are afraid). Many images of God are evident in our prayer. Classroom prayer can reinforce or challenge these images, promoting an image of God who is merciful, forgiving, understanding: a God of light, life, peace and hope. The nearness of God in Jesus can be communicated, as well as the otherness and majesty of the Father and the restless inspiration of the Holy Spirit. Trinitarian prayer will become natural to children and the image of God they form in their school prayer may well be the image that stays with them throughout the rest of their lives. The God to whom we pray is influential in the life we lead.

At the most basic level, how we think of God is shaped in the representations that we use. For instance, in prayer a teacher might use traditional representations of Christ like a crucifix, a Sacred Heart image, Holman Hunt's painting of Jesus as Light of the World, the Good Shepherd, or the Infant of Prague – each containing nuanced messages about who Jesus is (examples can be found using Google Image search). In the religious art of different cultures, Jesus is represented in a variety of ways which express aspects of these cultures. For example, Eastern European icons often show Jesus as an enthroned Byzantine emperor; South American depictions of Jesus often emphasis his simplicity and closeness to the oppressed poor whom he leads to freedom.

At the next level teachers might focus on the words we use in song and in prayer – and explore with children the different images of God that they portray. The formality or informality of our approach to God is significant (and it may vary from occasion to occasion). Finally, the kinds of things we say to God and ask of God are significant. If we call God 'Creator of heaven and earth' we evoke God's power and might, whereas if we call God 'Father of the poor' we evoke God's care for the disadvantaged – all in a title! The teacher must be conscious in preparing liturgy with children which image of God is being evoked.

Seasons, people and the world – keeping classroom prayer real

When children come to school they bring their home concerns with them. Their busy minds are full of ideas and their concerns can range from family to pets, friends and games. In class it can be quite a challenge to help them to focus on work or on prayer. It helps their concentration when the prayer is real. By 'real' we mean that if prayer emanates *from* their concerns and *expresses* these concerns then it is truly *their* prayer to God. For example:

> *Dear God,*
> *Sometimes I worry about not making friends at swimming. Please help me not to worry. Sometimes I worry about my little cousin Aidan because he was in hospital for a long time after he was born. Please help him. Sometimes I worry about my Granny because she is quite old. Please pray for her.*
> *Please help me with all my worries.*
> *Thank you God.*
> *Amen.*
> *(Maura Frances – aged 8)*

Three ways of keeping classroom and assembly prayer real are:

- praying the **seasons** of the year and of the Church
- praying for the **people** and relationships who make up their daily lives
- praying for the **world**; that is, the world beyond their own immediate experience, whether it be on another street or, indeed, continent.

Praying the seasons is relatively simple. It involves observing nature and bringing nature into the classroom through flowers, leaves, berries, fruits, bare branches etc. Advent, Christmas, Lent and Easter have their own rich symbolism that can be represented in the classroom, along with the colours associated with the liturgical cycle (e.g. purple for Advent, white for Christmas etc.). The whole appearance of the classroom can be changed in a way that evokes the season and affects the tone of the prayer. When the visual appearance of the prayer space is combined with appropriate music, seasonal words and liturgical actions, the resulting prayer can be very powerful.

When praying for people, the teacher's first exercise should be a listening one. What is of significance to the children? Who are the people who are important to them? Is someone ill or has someone died? Is there a new member of the family on the way? Have there been new friendships, fallings-out, new playground groups? Teachers need to be attentive to the people in a child's prayer. The child might open up in the reflective, prayerful environment in a way that they might not do at other times. A child might begin to cry whilst praying for someone, thereby indicating a level of emotion that the teacher should be aware of. If this happens the teacher will then comfort the child without drawing undue attention and then follow up, once the prayer is finished, by chatting with the child and providing appropriate support. It is healthy to balance prayers of intercession or asking for something with prayers of thanksgiving, so children do not just focus on asking God to help people in prayer, but also give thanks for the people who make up their lives.

In praying for the world, children become more aware of the needs of others and they also exercise generosity and openness by allowing themselves to be affected by the plight of people they have never met. In such a process prayer can enhance their awareness of their global citizenship. A sense of common humanity is encouraged and co-responsibility becomes their second nature. Here thanksgiving is important as well as praise to God, the Lord of all creation.

The creative process

So how does a teacher go about this process? How can this kind of positive, creative and engaging liturgy come about? There are a few key principles:

1. Involve the children from the start. Invite children to work with you from the start when preparing classroom prayer or school assemblies. Let them know that this will be something that will involve teamwork, where ideas will be shared and worked on together. At the very beginning ensure that the liturgy will be relevant to them by including them when deciding on the theme of the prayer. Quite often this discussion is very revealing as children share the issues that currently affect them and their community.

2. Be rooted in scripture. Liturgy provides the opportunity to communicate effectively with God. It is a two-way conversation so listening to God's Word as well as listening to each other should be at the heart of the prayer. Let scripture be at the centre of your liturgy. This can be done in two ways: a) Children can choose a theme for their prayer and then, with the help of their teacher, consider a suitable scripture reading as the basis from which to work; b) Choose a scripture passage from the outset, and then from this the theme and subsequent ideas will emerge. In choosing appropriate scripture passages with children, the gospels are often the most suitable to work with, especially gospel narrative and stories. In working with the Old Testament, stories are the most accessible parts to include in liturgy. Likewise with the gospels: for example, if children choose forgiveness as a theme for their prayer, the teacher could then suggest various suitable scriptural passages from which the children could choose, such as the story of the Prodigal Son (Luke 15:11-32), the Repentant Thief (Luke 23:41-43), or the Lost Sheep (Luke 15:4-7).

3. Respect Tradition. Children have great ideas (which sometimes need careful monitoring!) and using them to communicate the theme can be exciting and worthwhile. However, it is also important to respect tradition and to recognise appropriate opportunities to include well-known Church prayers and hymns. It is important for children to recognise, learn and understand traditional prayers and to appreciate that inclusion of them in a liturgy, alongside more creative and imaginative ways of praying, can add to the prayer experience.

4. Keep focused. Have one scriptural message or theme that the prayer develops. It is sometimes helpful for a phrase which reinforces the theme to be repeated throughout the prayer and this can be done in a variety of ways (said aloud, chanted, written on a banner etc.). For example, working again with the theme of forgiveness, the phrase 'God forgives us, so we forgive each other' could punctuate the liturgy at appropriate points. This means that the children ministering the prayer, and all who take part, are likely to leave the liturgy with the message clearly in mind.

5. Appealing to the senses. When prayer consists only of words, it easily becomes a mental exercise, engaging only the mind. Children in class or assembly are prone to loss of concentration, so the more they are engaged, the longer they are likely to remain involved. Appealing to the different senses in liturgy has a long history and involves such things as candles, bells, movement, incense, visual images, bread, wine, oil, music, rosary beads – and there is no reason this tradition cannot be built on in the school situation. Ensure that you build into each prayer-preparation session the question, 'How can we enhance this prayer by appealing to the senses'. Then watch the result! Returning to the theme of forgiveness, children might be invited to wash each others' hands, or place a pebble at the foot of a cross, symbolising the offering of their sins to God for forgiveness.

6. Don't be scared. While appropriateness is important, do not hold back. If the children are being creative in their suggestions then try them out. God speaks to us though the work we do, and even if some of the preparatory work for the liturgy is not used, the process of involving the children and participating in such work – based on the Word of God – is significant in itself.

Creative prayer with children is as much about the process as the final result. Creative prayer helps children 'own' their prayer. It can draw children closer to God and to each other. It can strengthen them for everyday life while nourishing spiritual life and encouraging spiritual growth. Creative prayer challenges adults to new ways of thinking about God and approaching God. Finally and most importantly it can form the children in a mature faith, focused on God and in touch with their real lives so that they become citizens of this world and of the Kingdom of God.

NOTES

1. Sacred Congregation for Catholic Education, *The Religious Dimension of Education in a Catholic School*, London: CTS, 1988, par. 83.
2. C. Maloney, F. O'Connell & B.T. O'Reilly, *Alive-O 7 Teachers' Book*, Dublin: Veritas, Publications, 2003, p. 21 (emphasis added).

Section Two
Chapter 2
Preparing the Way – Advent Prayer with Children: *themes, ideas and resources*

'Prepare the way of the Lord.'
John the Baptist (cf. Matthew 3:3)

Teacher's background knowledge – What does Advent mean?

Advent

Our first clue as to the meaning of Advent is the word itself: it is from the Latin version of the Our Father, 'Adveniat regnum tuum' – may your kingdom *'come'*. Advent celebrates the coming or arrival of Jesus Christ, at his birth in Bethlehem and his second coming at the end of time.

A season of joy and hope

John Paul II said: 'Advent … is a very evocative religious season because it is interwoven with hope and spiritual expectation: every time the Christian community prepares to commemorate the Redeemer's birth, it feels a quiver of joy which to a certain extent it communicates to the whole of society.' (St Peter's Square, 1st Sunday of Advent, 2005)

Our life is an Advent

John Paul II said:

The liturgy of Advent, filled with constant allusions to the joyful expectation of the Messiah, helps us **to understand the fullness of the value and meaning** *of the mystery of Christmas. It is not just about commemorating the historical event, which occurred some 2,000 years ago in a little village of Judea. Instead, we must understand that* **our whole life should be an "advent"**, *in vigilant expectation of Christ's final coming. To prepare our hearts to welcome the Lord who, as we say in the Creed, will come one day* *to judge the living and the dead, we must learn to recognise his presence in the events of daily life. Advent is then a **period of intense training** that directs us decisively to the One who has already come, who will come and who continuously comes.'* (Wednesday 18th December 2002, General Audience; emphasis added.)

The liturgy says:

> Lord, fill our hearts with your love,
> and as you revealed to us by an angel
> the coming of your Son as man,
> so lead us through his suffering and death
> to the glory of his resurrection,
> for he lives and reigns with you and the Holy Spirit,
> one God for ever and ever.

So:

> Advent is a season of joy
> Advent is a season of hope
> Advent is a time of watching and waiting
> Advent is a time of preparation
> Advent looks forward to Christmas
> Advent looks forward to the return of Christ at the end of time.

Key teaching points for children

What does Advent mean?
Advent means 'coming' or 'arrival'.

There are two important things we think about in Advent:

1. Jesus arrived into the world as a baby in the manger at Bethlehem. We are getting ready to celebrate his birthday.

2. Jesus promised he would return. We are getting ready for when Jesus comes again.

How long is Advent?

The length of Advent depends on what day Christmas falls on: Advent is the four Sundays before Christmas day and all the days in between. This means it begins around the end of November and ends on 24th December.

What is Advent like for us?

Advent is joyful – Jesus is our friend, and we look forward to meeting him.

Advent is a time of hope – having Jesus in our lives is always good.

Advent is a time of waiting – we pray that Jesus will come soon.

Advent is a time for preparing – Jesus is important and we want to be ready to meet him.

Jesus is with us every day – **Advent** is when we remember this.

Sample prayers

(P4–7 / 2nd–6th class)

> *Dear God,*
> *Thank you for Advent.*
> *It is our special time of preparing*
> *to meet Jesus your Son.*
> *Help us to get ready to meet him in our hearts.*
> *He is our special friend and he loves us.*
> *Help us to love him in the same way.*
> *Amen.*

(P1–3 / Junior Infants– 1st class)

> *Dear Jesus,*
> *We love you very much.*
> *We are getting ready for your birthday at Christmas.*
> *Please look after me;*
> *Please look after my family;*
> *Please look after everyone.*
> *Amen.*

Advent people: introducing Mary

'I am the handmaid of the Lord,' said Mary. 'Let what you have said be done to me.'
– Mary says 'Yes' to God (Luke 1:26-38)

'My soul proclaims the greatness of the Lord and my spirit rejoices in God my saviour.'
– Mary shares the Good News (Luke 1:39-56)

Mary – what some people said:
- She's too young to have a baby!
- She shouldn't be travelling while she's pregnant
- She claims she's had a vision
- Will Joseph stay with her?

Mary – what her friends said:
- She's so happy – she sings all the time!
- She'll be a brilliant mum
- Isn't it amazing – her cousin's expecting too!
- I've never seen faith so strong.

What she was really like:
An ordinary woman who believed the extraordinary promises of God: she was singled out to become the mother of God's Son. She was **obedient**, saying 'Yes' to God; she was **curious**, asking how these things could come to pass; she was **courageous**, stepping out into an uncertain future; she was **happy**, singing for joy at the promises of God; she was, in a sense, the **first apostle**, rushing to share the Good News that the Saviour was to be born (read Luke 1:26-56).

Prayer ideas

Telling the story (this section can be adapted for any Advent gospel)
- Tell the class you're going to read them a story which they will tell back to you.
- Read one of the two passages from Luke's gospel (for younger children use a children's bible). Emphasise that they must listen closely and try to remember the details.
- Ask one of the children to tell the story as they have heard it.
- After a couple of sentences, indicate to another child to take over the story. (From time to time allow other children to add omitted details.)
- For infants, give them a multiple choice; for example: The angel who came to Mary was called a) Wendy, b) Gareth, or c) Gabriel.

Mary cloth
The children make a patchwork cloth of blue materials; this 'Mary cloth' will be used in class prayer during Advent.
- Ask children to bring in a square of blue cloth (e.g. 15cmx15cm – for younger children, send home a square cardboard template for parents to use.)
- The cloth can be patterned or plain, as long as it contains the colour blue.
- Depending on the age of the class, you or a group of children can stitch the patches together to create a larger cloth. (This can continue over a number of days.)

The result is a 'Mary cloth', a gift created for Mary by the class, to let her know that she is loved for being the mother of Jesus and for bringing him into the world.

Advent people: introducing John the Baptist

'Prepare a way for the Lord, make his path straight.'
– John instructs us to prepare for the coming of God (Mark 1:1-8)

'I have baptised you with water, but he will baptise you with the Holy Spirit.'
– John proclaims the greatness of Jesus (Mark 1:1-8)

John: what some people said:
- He shouts a lot and he's scary
- He looks a bit rough
- He must be very strict
- What is he trying to do?

John: what his friends said:
- He's a powerful preacher
- He's not afraid of anyone
- He's so holy
- He's got great faith.

What he was really like:
John was a **messenger** for God, like a **prophet** from the Old Testament, preaching about the need to repent and be sorry for sins. He was **fearless** in his preaching, and lived a **simple** life, wearing rough clothes and not eating much. He told the people that they must **prepare** the way of the Lord, get ready for the Messiah. He helped them to prepare by **baptising** them in the River Jordan. He was **humble**, making way for Jesus.

Prayer ideas

Who was John the Baptist?

Read the story of John the Baptist to the children (Mark 1:1-8). Divide the children into groups. Have each group draw round one child, making a body-shape on paper. Provide them with wool, bits of cloth and other materials from the junk box. Ask them to decorate the shape so it looks like John the Baptist (e.g. long hair and beard, rough clothes). One of these decorated figures can then be used in liturgy, where the focus is on John's character and his message. During a liturgy, invite the children to suggest words that describe what John looked like (e.g. scruffy, long-haired) and write these words around the figure of John. Then ask the children to suggest what John's character was like (e.g. fearless, loud), and write these words in a different coloured pen. Finally, invite the children to suggest things John might have said when he was preaching (e.g. God is great; Prepare) and write these down in a third colour.

Liturgy of Preparing

Explain to the children that you are now going to pray together and get ready for the coming of Jesus.

Getting ready on the outside

Invite the children to mime washing their hands, and ask them to say, 'Help me to be ready, Jesus'. Invite the children to mime combing or brushing their hair, and ask them to say, 'Help me to be good when you come'. Invite the children to mime washing their faces, and ask them to say, 'Help me to be happy when you come'. Older children could simply be invited to wash their hands in a bowl of water, whilst saying, 'Help me to be ready, Jesus, when you come'.

Getting ready on the inside

Invite the children to think of any way they might have hurt their families or friends. Then ask them to say in turn, 'I am sorry'.

Invite the children to think how they might be good, and to say in turn, 'I will try to be good'.

Say an Advent Prayer (*the children repeat line by line after the teacher*):
> *Dear Jesus,*
> *help us get ready for Christmas*
> *by being good*
> *by being kind*
> *and by helping each other.*
> *Amen. **(Infants)***
>
> *Dear Jesus*
> *John the Baptist told us to get ready*
> *and prepare a way for the Lord.*
> *Help us to do as he says*
> *so we can welcome you into our hearts,*
> *now, at Christmas, and always.*
> *Amen. **(Older children)***

Advent people: introducing Joseph and the Angel Gabriel

Joseph
'When Joseph woke up, he did what the angel of the Lord had told him to do. He took his wife to his home.'
– Joseph believed in the goodness of God (Matthew 1:18-24)

What was Joseph really like?
Joseph was a working man, a carpenter. He loved Mary very much, and was protective of her. He was frightened when he heard she was to have a child, but he was reassured in a dream that it was all God's plan, and accepted God's will. He carried out his role, looking after both Mary and Jesus.

The Angel Gabriel
'The Angel Gabriel was sent by God to a town in Galilee called Nazareth.'
– Gabriel is God's messenger (Luke 1:26-38)

'Rejoice, so highly favoured, the Lord is with you.'
– Gabriel is a bringer of good news.

What was Gabriel really like?
Gabriel was God's **messenger**. The name Gabriel means 'God is my strength' or 'The strength of God'. Gabriel appears in the Old Testament (Daniel 8:16-26), to Mary, and to Zechariah, the father of John the Baptist (Luke 1:11-20). Gabriel silences Zechariah for his lack of faith.

Prayer ideas

Praying with Joseph: A simple crib
When returning home, Joseph would have made a crib for the baby Jesus. We are going to use cardboard, pieces of twig (or lollipop sticks) and glue to make a simple crib. A larger version of the crib could be used in classroom liturgy.

Instructions

Cut out an A5 piece of cardboard. Glue a twig along each long edge of the card. Next, glue a twig along each short edge of the card, resting on the ends of the first twigs. Continue to do this, building up a basket effect with the twigs. Line the completed crib with cloth or cotton wool.

Praying with Gabriel

The Angel Gabriel brought God's message to us. Let's send our messages to God.

Instructions

Cut out a feather shape (see page 125 for template) for each member of the class. Invite the children to write a message to God, and decorate the feather. This message can tell God anything the children want to tell. If a child is shy about sharing his or her message, allow them to decorate over it. During a liturgy or class prayer, place a large angel (based on the template on page 126) on the floor or on the wall, and invite the children to send their messages to God by sticking their message-feathers on the wings of the angel. You can close the liturgy by leading the children line-by-line in the following prayer:

> *Angel of God,*
> *You carried the good news to Mary and to us.*
> *We ask you to take our messages to God.*
> *We love him very much.*

Working with the Word

The Advent readings, especially the gospels, are our chief resource in preparing liturgies and classroom prayers. The first step in prayer is to make these readings accessible to children. We use the Word (scripture passage) in four ways:

- **explore** the Word
- **present** the Word
- **reflect** on the Word
- **respond** to the Word.

Prepare a reading in advance – it will be easier and more fruitful when you're working with children, producing liturgy. Here is a 4-step approach you can use:

Step 1 Ask yourself 'What kind of scripture passage is this?' – is it a story, a teaching, a parable? Is it meant to inform, inspire, warn …

Step 2 Examine the text; read it slowly to yourself, preferably out loud. Look at each word, notice every detail. What is the reading saying? What do you learn from it? How does it make you feel?

Step 3 Look for themes; write down as many as you can. Underline the most important themes. Select a theme you will use for a liturgy or classroom prayer.

Step 4 Think of different ways in which this reading can be presented to the children and by the children (see below), so that its meaning is made clearer. When you have chosen a way of presenting the reading, work with the children to bring the Word alive. Always include a simple, direct presentation of the Word so that the meaning is not lost.

Presenting the Word

Dialogue – imagine (and write down) a conversation between two characters in the gospel passage (for example) you are using; let the meaning of the text come through the dialogue.

Eye-witness – Prepare an eye-witness account of an incident in the reading – let the children imagine they were there, and tell the story in their own words.

Litany – Adapt the reading you are using into a litany, with a refrain which is repeated after each phrase; or adapt the reading into the form of a prayer.

Reflection – Tell the story or repeat the teaching in the reading in a reflective, meditative way which encourages children to understand it more deeply.

Poem – A poem based on the reading can communicate its meaning for children.
Interview – A news interviewer asks those who were there what they saw and heard.

Prayer ideas

Here we explore the presentation of an Advent gospel – the Visitation, where Mary journeys to see her cousin Elizabeth to share with her the good news she has received (Luke 1:39-45, Advent Gospel 21st December).

Reflect on the passage using the four steps suggested above. **Work with the children in bringing the Word alive**. The following are examples, for guidance.

Dialogue

A dialogue can form the main part of a liturgy or classroom prayer as there is scope for telling the whole of the reading.

Elizabeth: What a lovely surprise, Mary. I'm so glad to see you. I have lots of news!

Mary: I've got news too! You won't believe it!

Elizabeth: Well, let's sit down and have a good chat. Tell me your news first.

Mary: OK. I was sitting at home when an angel came to me. The angel was called Gabriel, and told me I was going to have God's son!

Elizabeth: Really? That is amazing. Were you afraid?

Mary: Yes, at first. But the angel put my mind at rest. He told me so much, I keep going over it in my head so I don't forget it.

Elizabeth: Tell me more about the baby.

Mary: Well, the baby is going to be called Jesus. He is going to be a powerful ruler.

Elizabeth: That's the most wonderful thing ever! *(The dialogue continues).*

Eye-witness

This account is based on the scripture passage, but can include details supplied by the imagination of the children.

'I saw Mary the other day, setting off from her house to see her cousin Elizabeth. She looked as if she was in a real hurry, so I walked with her for a while, to see if I could help her. She told me the most amazing story about what had happened to her. I could hardly believe it, but I know she always tells the truth, so it must be true. A messenger from God came to see her – an angel called Gabriel. He told her she had been picked out specially to have God's son. As she was telling me this, her eyes were shining, as though the angel was still there. It made me so happy to hear her. She was hurrying because she was so excited. And she had heard news about Elizabeth too: even though Elizabeth was quite old, she was expecting a baby! I decided then that I would walk with Mary all the way to Elizabeth's house, to keep her company. She was delighted, and we talked all the way. When we reached Elizabeth's … *(The eye-witness account continues).*

Litany

Litanies can include a story from scripture, or can relate to themes. This example tells the story:

You listened to the angel

   Response: Hail Mary, full of grace

You accepted God's will

You rushed to share your good news

You told your cousin Elizabeth

She said you are blessed

She was so happy for you

Her own baby jumped for joy inside her

You stayed with Elizabeth

Together you prayed to God *(The litany continues).*

Reflection

A quiet exercise, with peaceful music on in the background.

Close your eyes, and sit comfortably. Imagine you are Mary. You are sitting in your house all by yourself. You have just heard amazing news from the angel Gabriel. The angel has just left you, and you are so excited that you are going to have a baby who is God's son. Who can you tell? The first person you think of is your cousin Elizabeth, so you pack a bag and head off to meet her. It's a long walk, so you set off early in the morning, before it gets too hot. You walk on the road, and it is dusty and noisy until you leave the town. In the countryside it is nice and quiet. As you walk, you think again of what the angel has said, and what God is doing for you, and for everyone. You keep saying over and over again, 'Thank you God' *(The reflection continues).*

Poem

It is often possible to use more than one poem in a liturgy or classroom prayer. When poems are prepared in groups, they frequently turn out quite differently from each other. Different approaches strengthen the communication of the message.

Mary heard the angel, who told her she was blest
She wanted to tell someone, Elizabeth was best
She packed up her bag and went on her way
She wanted to arrive there the very same day
She walked on the road, not feeling any fear
After a few hours, Elizabeth's was quite near
She knocked on the door, with a smile on her face
Elizabeth was surprised, held Mary in an embrace *(The poem continues).*

Interview

The interview can take the form of a chat show or news report. The interviewer has to draw the story from the interviewee by asking relevant questions.

Interviewer: Hello, can you please tell us your name and where you're from?

Mary: My name is Mary, and I'm from Nazareth.

Interviewer: We hear that strange things have been happening to you, Mary. Are the reports true?

Mary: That depends on what you've heard! I was visited by an angel, and given some amazing news. I set off to share this news with my cousin.

Interviewer: For the sake of listeners at home, your cousin is Elizabeth: is that correct?

Mary: That's right, and she has her own story to tell too.

Interviewer: We'll have to arrange to interview her later! *(Interview continues).*

Make a joyful noise: music for Advent

Advent is the Season of:

1. **The minor key.** If you have a knowledge of music, you'll know what this means. If not, think of music that is haunting, even sad; subdued, solemn. Examples in classical music would be Fantasia on a Theme of Thomas Tallis by Vaughan Williams.

Think of typical hymns during Advent and how they sound: 'O come, O come, Emmanuel'; 'The Angel Gabriel from heaven came.'

2. **Silence.** Advent is not a time of exuberance, but of quiet preparation. Silence can be used effectively. A simple chant (see page 42) is often a good way to introduce silence, and draw it to a close.

3. **Reflection and meditation.** Mary did not at first understand what the Angel Gabriel told her; she needed to absorb the full impact of the news she had received: 'She asked herself what this greeting could mean' (read Luke 1:29). Music for Advent will usually be thoughtful rather than celebratory.

Principles

- **Keep it simple** – simple inclusions can be incredibly effective: any noise is joyful to God.

- **Rooted in scripture** – when scripture is at the heart of the music or sound, the message of God will be heard.

- **Make it up!** – if you have an idea, don't hold back.

- **Keep focused** – let the music follow the theme.

- **Work with the children's ideas** – allow the children to create (which also makes it easier for you!)

- **Liturgy can be fun!** – don't be afraid of laughter and smiles in the right places!

- **Include action** – make up actions (with the children) to go with the words and music.

Ways of using sound

Song (traditional and new); Chant; Instruments (melodic); Percussion; Silence; CDs (for listening to and for background); Natural noises.

Prayer ideas

Sound Story

(This activity can be implemented during a lesson and the result could be included in a liturgy or class prayer time.)

- In groups the children can read one of the Advent stories, for example, the Annunciation (read Luke 1:26-38).

- Have a selection of percussion instruments for each group (chimes, bell, gong, rattle, drum, xylophone etc.).

- Invite the children to choose sounds to represent the significant stages of the story (for example, the chimes could be played three times to represent the arrival of the Angel Gabriel).

- The children should practice this with someone reading the story aloud to ensure that they have the sounds in the correct sequence.

- Finally, the words of the story are dropped and only the instruments are used, creating an effective Advent sound story. The children can present these to the rest of the class and children should try to recognise the different stages in the story. One of the sound stories could be used during prayer.

Differentiation

With children who are musically more able, invite them to include their own non-percussion instrument in the story.

For younger children, have fewer and easier instruments. Perhaps work as a class, focusing on words instead of phrases in the story. At the end, the words of the story can be kept when working with younger children.

Advent Chant

- Choose any phrase from Advent scripture or make up an appropriate one yourself (e.g. 'He shall be called Emmanuel' or 'We are waiting for you, Lord').
- Choose a note, any note that is in your head and sing the phrase to this single note.
- This time vary the tune by going up a note or down a note (or both) at some point in the phrase – you can't go wrong!
- Sing it to the children, inviting them to repeat. (This can be sung 5– 10 times.)
- When chanting, vary the dynamics by getting louder and quieter. It can be effective to finish the chant by singing it very quietly, and then follow this with a period of prayerful silence.
- Older children: give an example and then ask them to create their own simple chant (encourage them to look at the Advent gospels and choose or adapt an appropriate phrase).
- A simple chant like this can be used once, or at several points throughout a liturgy.

The Waiting Prayer

This prayer focuses on the Advent theme of *watching* and *waiting*.

During a liturgy, tell the children that they have to wait in silence until they hear the sound of a percussion instrument. Encourage them to focus on the waiting. When the sound comes, they should all pray out loud the phrase, 'Hail Mary, full of grace'. This can happen five or six times, alternating the length of time between waiting. (The teacher can lead this at first but then invite a child to lead this waiting prayer.)

New words to old hymns

Pick a simple (non-Advent) hymn the children know, and allow the children to work in groups writing new, Advent-themed words. Let them listen to each other's compositions, and allow them to choose which ones are to be used in their liturgy (perhaps by vote).

For example, to the tune of 'Peace Perfect Peace':

Lord, we will wait, you are coming to us soon (x2)
We are your children, we long to welcome you
Lord, we will wait, you are coming to us soon.

Mother of Jesus, you are the special one (x2)
We want to thank you: we're waiting for your Son
Mother of Jesus, you are the special one.

To the tune of 'Be Still and Know I am with You':

We're waiting for your coming
We're watching for you, Lord.
The Angel Gabriel's spoken,
You're coming to this world,
Jesus.

Mary, you are so special
You said 'Yes' to the Lord.
Thank you for bringing us Jesus
We praise your name aloud,
Most Blessed.

Decorate, make and pray

Advent is Purple
The colour traditionally associated with Advent is **purple** or **violet** – not so much penitential as in Lent, but rather a **watchful, reflective, sober** colour. It is the quiet, calm period before the bright celebration of Christmas. The purple (violet) will give way to the white and silver of Christmas.

Advent is Pink
The 3rd Sunday of Advent is known traditionally as **Gaudete** Sunday (from the Latin, meaning **Rejoice**). This is because the readings from St Paul begin with Rejoice, be happy. So the colour changes from purple (violet) to **pink** (rose).

Advent is Austere
As a time of preparation, Advent is characterised by **simplicity**. Decorations of your classroom prayer space should be **austere**, not showy as befits Christmas. Rather than using flowers, for example, use greenery. Evergreens are popular in Advent (e.g. holly, spruce, yew). Candles can be purple (or pink). John the Baptist preached in the desert wilderness, so a classroom desert **wilderness** could be created with sand and stones.

Advent is Watching and Waiting
Symbols of **watchfulness** emphasise this aspect of the season, e.g. alarm clocks, binoculars. The traditional Advent wreath is useful in highlighting the progression of the Season. The Jesse tree can be adapted to reinforce themes you will be focusing on in Advent.

Advent is Light in Darkness
We celebrate Christmas in the middle of winter, which is for us the darkest time of the year. So our Advent preparation is longing for the light which is Christ to shine into our world. A purple candle could represent our waiting for Jesus. A green candle could represent the whole of nature waiting for Jesus – our prayer for the world; a red candle could represent the suffering Jesus would face in his life – and those who are suffering in the world; a white candle could represent the hope Jesus brings to the world – all our longings and expectations. Children could choose which candle is lit at the beginning of each liturgy, depending on the focus they would like, whether praying for themselves, for the world, for those who are suffering.

Prayer ideas

The Advent Wreath

The traditional Advent wreath is a circle of greenery with five candles: three purple, one pink and one white (to be lit at Christmas). This has long been popular in classroom prayer. An adapted version could include:

- Different coloured candles as suggested above
- A living wreath: during a liturgy, children form a circle and hold hands to create the wreath. A child (or children, or the teacher) could stand in the middle and read an Advent prayer
- A floor wreath: a large circle of cardboard, decorated with cut-out leaves. This can be used in classroom prayer, with children sitting around it. Its use can be adapted: for example, placing written prayers into it.

Near and Far – praying with binoculars

During classroom prayer, sit children in a circle, and pass round a pair (or more than one pair) of binoculars. Invite the children to look through the binoculars at a picture of Jesus firstly from the wrong end of the lens. The picture seems smaller and further away. Then invite them to look the correct way, and see how it comes closer. Draw out from this exercise the watching and waiting for Jesus – how each day of Advent we celebrate Jesus coming closer and closer.

Blink

Play the traditional game of Blink where the children stand in a circle. One child is secretly nominated as the 'blinker'. This child eliminates other children in the circle by blinking at them; when a child has been 'blinked at' they sit down. One child stands in the centre of the circle and has to identify the 'blinker' as soon as possible. Three false accusations, and the 'blinker' has won.

   Link this game with the teaching of Jesus in Mark 13:33-37 where Jesus advises his disciples to be on their guard, to be watchful and not caught unawares when Jesus returns. The game Blink encourages this watchfulness.

Advent Prayer Clock

Make a large classroom clock from cardboard – the clock should have just one hand. At the centre of the clock face, put a large star. This is the star that guided the Wise Men on their long journey to find the infant Jesus. Each number on the clock represents a prayer intention for Advent; these intentions can be shown by putting a picture at each number. Intentions could include some of the following: *family, school, hungry children, friends, peace, world, homeless people, unemployed people, sick people, the dead, the old, the young, babies, priests, teachers, the head-teacher*!

This clock can be used for morning prayer (or at other times) and the focus of the prayer can be decided by the class each day, or by the clockwise progression of the hand. The prayer can be introduced each day by saying, 'Let the Advent star guide us to Jesus as we pray for …'

Advent readings at a glance

Year A

1st Sunday of Advent	Isaiah 2:1-5	Romans13:11-14
	Matthew 24:37-44	
	Stay awake so you may be ready	

2nd Sunday of Advent	Isaiah 11:1-10	Romans 15:4-9
	Matthew 3:1-12	
	Repent	

3rd Sunday of Advent	Isaiah 35:1-6, 10	James 5:7-10
	Matthew 11:2-11	
	Are you the one who is to come?	

4th Sunday of Advent	Isaiah 7:10-14	Romans 1:1-7
	Matthew 1:18-24	
	Jesus was born of Mary	

Year B

1st Sunday of Advent	Isaiah 63:16-17; 64:1, 3-8	1 Corinthians 1:3-9
	Mark 13:33-37	
	Stay awake	

2nd Sunday of Advent	Isaiah 40:1-5, 9-11	2 Peter 3:8-14
	Mark 1:1-8	
	Make his paths straight	

3rd Sunday of Advent	Isaiah 61:1-2, 10-11	1Thessalonians 5:16-24
	John 1:6-8, 19-28	
	I am not fit to undo his sandal strap	

4th Sunday of Advent	Samuel 7:1-5, 8-12, 14, 16	Romans 16:25-27
	Luke 1:26-38	
	You are to conceive and bear a son	

Year C

| 1st Sunday of Advent | Jeremiah 33:14-16 | 1 Thessalonians 3:12-4:2 |

Luke 21:25-28, 34-36
Your liberation is near at hand

| 2nd Sunday of Advent | Baruch 5:1-9 | Philippians 1:3-6, 8-11 |

Luke 3:1-6
All mankind shall see the salvation of God

| 3rd Sunday of Advent | Zephaniah 3:14-18 | Philippians 4:4-7 |

Luke 3:10-18
What must we do?

| 4th Sunday of Advent | Micah 5:1-4 | Hebrews 10:5-10 |

Luke 1:39-44
Why should I be honoured with this visit?

Chapter 3
Getting Ready – Lenten Prayer with Children: *themes, ideas and resources*

'Getting Ready' follows on from the last chapter, 'Preparing the Way'. It is a creative resource to support teachers in their own faith, it helps teachers imaginatively communicate this faith to the children they teach, and it encourages both teacher and children to be creative when they pray.

Each section of this chapter is in two parts: 'Reminding the Teacher' and 'Praying with Children'.

(a)   Reminding the Teacher
- We look at one of the Lenten gospel readings
- The significance of the gospel is spelled out
- We use the reading in our own prayer
- We reflect on one main theme for our classroom prayer with children.

(b)   Praying with Children
- Exploring the theme with children
- Suggestions for prayer activities including word, music, symbol, movement
- Resources for classroom prayer.

Why the fuss about Lent?
Lent is the season leading up to Easter. The word 'Lent' comes from the Old English, 'Lengcthen', referring to the lengthening of the daylight hours in Spring, after the darkness of Winter.

A major theme of Lent comes from the Prophet Baruch. God says to the people of Israel, and now to us, 'Come back to me with all your hearts'.

Forty Days
Traditionally Lent is forty days, echoing the forty days spent by Jesus in the wilderness (or desert), where he was tempted by Satan, and prepared for his public

ministry. If you count the days from Ash Wednesday (the beginning of Lent) to Easter Sunday, it adds up to more than forty days; this is because Sundays, on which Christians always celebrate the resurrection of Jesus, are not counted as days of Lenten penance (see below).

Lenten Penance – Prayer, Fasting and Almsgiving

From the earliest years of the Church, Lent is a time of Prayer, Fasting and Almsgiving. We pray, asking God for the help and strength we need for our Christian lives. We fast, abstaining from excessive consumption to discipline ourselves. And we give alms, offerings of money, goods or time to those less well-off than ourselves.

Shrove Tuesday

The day before Lent begins is traditionally called 'Shrove Tuesday'. This name comes from the Old English verb 'to shrive', which means 'to absolve'. So Shrove Tuesday was the last opportunity for Christians to make their confession and receive absolution before beginning their Lenten penance. Shrove Tuesday is also popularly known as 'Pancake Tuesday'. It is the day when households used up eggs, sugar and milk before the fasting of Ash Wednesday and Lent. Linked with this last-minute indulgence before the austerity of Lent is the custom in many countries of 'Carnevale' (from where we derive our word 'carnival'). It is made up of two words, 'Carne' which is Latin for meat, and 'Vale' which is a farewell greeting. So Carnevale is a festival of celebration, before belts are tightened for Lent.

Ash Wednesday

Ash Wednesday marks the formal beginning of Lent. From Old Testament times, the faithful would daub themselves with ash to show they were penitent – like make-up in reverse, making themselves unattractive, turning from prevailing custom. On Ash Wednesday the liturgy of the Church advises Catholics to 'Turn from sin, believe the Good News'. An older form of the imposition of the ashes refers back to the creation of Adam from dust by God in the book of Genesis: 'Remember that you are dust, and unto dust you will return.'

Alleluia – not a Lent word!

Lent gains its meaning by the way it prepares us for and points us towards Easter. It is the fast before the feast. During Lent, one word is conspicuously absent from the official liturgy of the Church – Alleluia. This is because Alleluia is a one-word prayer or acclamation welcoming the Risen Christ, so we do not use it whilst recalling the temptation, suffering and death of Jesus, but we sing it out loud and clear at the Easter Vigil, Easter Masses, and throughout the rest of the year. Gospel Acclamations during Lent omit Alleluia, and instead begin with 'Praise to you, O Christ, King of eternal glory' or other acclamations based on Lent readings.

So to recap:

- Lent is our identification with Our Lord's temptations in the wilderness (desert)
- Lent has its roots in the Old Testament
- Lent is an austere time, a time of self-denial and prayer
- Lent is a preparation for the Feast of Easter
- Traditionally we 'give things up' for Lent
- Traditionally we pray more during Lent
- Traditionally we increase our efforts to help those worse off than ourselves
- The focus in Lent is on the ministry of John the Baptist, preparing the way for Jesus
- The focus in Lent is on the trials and sufferings of Jesus
- The focus in Lent is preparing us for the death of Jesus, and the resurrection which is to come.

Opening up the Word

The Word is central to Christian prayer

The Bible is a library, a collection of many works of literature spanning centuries; it includes history, prophecy, poetry, testimony, visionary writing, biography. The basic division of the Bible is into the Old Testament, the Hebrew scriptures up to the time of Jesus, and the New Testament, from the four gospels to the Book of Revelation. In the book, this is literature; when it is proclaimed and lived, it is a living Word, the Word of God. It is the core literature of the Christian community, where we learn about God, about ourselves and about the world, and as such is utterly central to Christian prayer. When we pray by ourselves to God, we call God Father, as we have learned to do from the Word; we pray to Jesus, whom the Word reveals to be the only Son of the Father; and we pray in the Holy Spirit, whom Jesus sent at Pentecost. When we pray together, we gather around the Word, celebrate the Word, reflect on the Word, and think about how we can put the Word into action in our lives.

- The Word is at the root of prayer
- The Word resources prayer
- The Word deepens prayer
- The Word informs prayer.

Reading, absorbing, reflecting, discussing, listening – all ways of 'hearing' the Word. This is true for you, and true for children too.

Where do we begin?

Here we will take one of the gospels for Lent, look at the rich variety of themes it contains, themes that can be explored and developed in classroom prayer. The simplest way of doing this is to read the passage word by word, line by line, seeing what is being said, picking out possible themes, and then relating them to children. For example, in the passage below, the first theme we come across is the Spirit compelling Jesus to go out into the wilderness; for children, we would talk about the power of the Holy Spirit (a good theme particularly for a Confirmation class).

The Spirit drove Jesus out into the wilderness and he remained there for forty days, and he was tempted by Satan. He was there with the wild beasts and the angels looked after him.

After John had been arrested, Jesus went into Galilee. There he proclaimed the Good News from God. 'The time has come,' he said, 'and the kingdom of God is close at hand. Repent and believe the Good News.' Mark 1:12-15

Themes

- The power of the Holy Spirit
- The wilderness: taking time out to pray
- Resisting temptation
- Being looked after by God (guardian angels)
- John is arrested – believing in God is not always easy
- Jesus is a teacher
- God's Good News
- The time has come – Jesus is already with us, here and now
- We are very close to heaven
- Saying sorry
- Believe the Good News – trust in God.

Now you try!

Now try identifying the themes in another familiar gospel passage, where Jesus is teaching the disciples how to pray. We have come up with thirteen themes – can you do better than us? You'll find them at the end of this chapter (page 84). But no cheating!

> *'Our Father in heaven,*
> *May your name be held holy,*
> *Your kingdom come,*
> *Your will be done on earth as it is in heaven.*
> *Give us today our daily bread.*
> *And forgive us our debts,*
> *As we have forgiven those who are in debt to us.*
> *And do not put us to the test,*
> *But save us from the evil one.'*
> Matthew 6:9-13

Opening up the scriptures in this way will help stimulate creativity in preparing classroom prayer, give you a way of working which ensures the Word of God is central to this prayer, and makes the scriptures accessible to children.

Children in the upper school can be encouraged to work with you in identifying themes from scripture. Don't be put off by difficult passages – working together can produce exciting, even unexpected results. Resist the temptation to control the outcome too much!

Desert

'The Spirit drove Jesus into the desert.'
Mark 1:12-15

(a)   Reminding the Teacher

Why this reading?

The Spirit drives Jesus into the desert (or 'wilderness') to help him focus on the spiritual conflict in which he is engaged – he is to proclaim God's kingdom, and will be opposed by evil. Jesus steps aside from his normal, everyday life to concentrate on what is going on inside him. Traditionally, this is how Christians approach Lent. We step aside from our normal, everyday lives to strengthen ourselves spiritually. We don't stop work or alter our daily routine radically, but we do make more time for God.

What does it say?

Jesus, being driven by the Spirit, is allowing himself to be led by God. He knows there are trials he must face, and he knows the mission he is to accomplish is given to him by his Father, so he obeys the Spirit. Even though he is in a wild, abandoned place, God still looks after him. Life elsewhere continues, and John the Baptist is arrested and will be put to death for proclaiming the truth – a hint of what will happen to Jesus. John's passing marks the beginning of Jesus' mission – the Old Testament represented by John prepared the way for Jesus; now Jesus is here, the New Testament begins and Jesus himself announces the Good News. 'Repent,' Jesus says – a word which means 'turn around'. If you are facing the wrong way, turn back to God.

Main points to communicate to children

- Jesus was obedient to his heavenly Father
- Lent is a time when we pray more
- We can always turn back to God
- God will look after us
- If we really try hard, we can resist temptation.

Reminder

Lent is not just a duty, it has a real purpose. During Lent we are imitating Jesus so we might be spiritually strengthened and reconciled to God.

Teacher's Prayer

Why not say this prayer every day for the next week?

> *Heavenly Father*
> *As the Holy Spirit drove Jesus out into the desert*
> *may I too obey your will.*
> *Let me be open to your promptings in my heart,*
> *let me turn from sin and believe the Good News,*
> *let me believe your kingdom is close at hand*
> *and let me share with others all that you have given me.*
> *I ask this through Jesus your Son,*
> *Amen.*

(b)   Praying with Children

Prayer desert

Claim an area of earth in the playground (about 3mx3m) and if possible cover it in wet sand (a bag of sand can bought cheaply from a local DIY store). If there is no sand, just use the earth. Invite the children to bring in a stone or pebble which will be called their 'sorry stone'. During a prayer service, invite the children to hold the cold stone in their hand and lead them in a meditation telling them that this represents the things that they have done that they are sorry for. Remind them of how much Jesus loves them even when they are sometimes naughty. Tell them that they are going to go outside and place their stone in their prayer desert. The stones will be placed together to form a cross, reminding us that Jesus died to take away all the things we do that are wrong.

Prayer circle

Create a classroom desert in which prayer can take place. Much of this involves the children's imagination but the space can be claimed by arranging stones in a large circle. (If not stones, string or fabric can be tied together to create the large circle.) Before the prayer begins, the children are invited into the circle; when they enter it they are in their special space.

With infants, help them imagine Jesus' desert experience by using visual props (pictures of cacti, lion, camel, snake, scorpion, locusts).

Prayer Mix and Match

Create a prayer that can be said together at every prayer session in Lent. Use a very simple structure such as:

- Name God
- Say what God has done
- Ask for something
- Thanks for God's action
- Amen.

Have a variety of suggestions for each part of the prayer and every day these could be mixed and matched. For example, for 'Name of God' we could have, *Loving Father; Jesus, Son of God; Jesus, Prince of Peace; Lord; Father in Heaven.* If you have a bank of suggestions for each part of the prayer then these can be displayed and every morning a child can select from each of the different parts and read out the prayer. Here is a finished example for an upper stages/older class:

Father in Heaven
Creator of us all
Help us each day of our lives to remain faithful to you
Thank you for your love.
Amen.

For young infants, pictures could be used to represent each part of the prayer and the teacher writes the caption underneath. In the same way as before, a child can be invited to choose a picture from each section of the prayer and the teacher reads out each caption and the children repeat. Probably five examples of each section would be appropriate.

Holy Spirit feather prayer

Using a real feather (for example, from a pillow) or a handmade tissue feather, invite a child to stand on a chair (be aware of safety) and to raise the feather as high as possible above the head. When the child lets it go and until it reaches the ground, the class silently pray to the Holy Spirit, making their petition. This short and effective prayer can punctuate a prayer service. A variation is for the class to pray together, *'Holy Spirit guide us'* as they watch the feather fall gently to the ground.

Gift box

Invite the children to come up with ten or so positive actions that they could do during Lent. (For example: smile; speak to someone who's lonely; tidy your desk; tidy your room; say a prayer for someone who needs it; say something kind; let someone else go first.) Print each of their suggestions on a piece of card, making two of each. During a prayer service invite each child to come forward and pick out a positive action for the day. They keep this action secret. This task could be done at the start of each day, during morning prayer. The children are invited to come forward group by group, they stand in a line, select their task, look at it, put it back in and return to their desk. This need not be time consuming and the children start each day knowing that this task will be pleasing to God. (A variation for infants or less able children is to have the tasks illustrated pictorially and explain what each picture means before inviting the children to choose.)

Do Without day

Each child chooses some everyday non-necessity to do without for a day; while they are doing without it, they offer a prayer for those who are hungry. During prayer the next day, children are invited to say who they prayed for and what they went without (a TV programme, computer game, listening to music, sweets, favourite food, staying up late, favourite item of clothing). The children will have many other examples!

Percussion in prayer

Using only percussion instruments, invite the children to suggest sounds that would represent the wind and the blowing sand of the desert. During prayer time, a group of children could play the rehearsed desert sounds, and the simple prayer, *'Thank you Jesus for your love'* can be repeated at the beginning and end.

Silence

Encourage periods of silence during a class service, allowing the children some time for personal prayer. Jesus spent much time in the desert praying and he would have been silent for much of this. Silence is something that the children should be exposed to gradually and could be lengthened by a few seconds each time it is introduced. What comes before the silence is important. Don't expect the children to respect this if they have just sung an upbeat song or been involved in a lively drama! Try introducing periods of silence after some reflective music or a reflection/meditation (see 'Reflection' below).

New words

As a class, and based on the theme of this week, invite the children to come up with new words to the well-known hymn, 'Father We Adore You'. Once these words have been written, the children can learn them and then sing the new words as a round (e.g. half the children sing the first line, and then when they start singing the second line, the other half of the children start to sing the first line, and so on). Even young children can take part in creating the new words! Here is an example:
'Led by the Spirit, you pray in the desert. Help us Jesus.'

Reflection

This quiet exercise brings the Word of God alive for the children. Invite them to sit calmly and have some peaceful music on in the background. Read each part of the refection and have long pauses in between, particularly if you are inviting them to imagine something.

'Close your eyes and sit comfortably. Imagine you are Jesus. You have been in the desert for four days and you are all alone. You have been walking for a few hours today and although there is a soft breeze it is still very warm. You stop walking and sit down for a rest. What does it look like in the desert? What colours can you see? You have not met anyone for days but many creatures have crossed your path. What kinds of animals or insects can you see? Are they friendly or dangerous? Everything is very peaceful where you are sitting and you close your eyes. You listen to the noises around you. There is hardly a sound except for the gentle wind and some insects chatting. You are so happy to be able to relax in this place. You know that your life is going to be very busy over the next few weeks and it scares you. You think of your Father in Heaven and you start to pray to him. What do you ask him for? What do you say? …' (*The reflection continues*). Gently bring the children out of the meditation at the end, and say a simple prayer together.

Glory

'His face shone like the sun and his clothes became as white as the light.'
Matthew 17:1-9
(The Transfiguration)

(a)   Reminding the Teacher

Why this reading?
The scripture readings during Lent lead up to the celebration of Jesus' suffering and death, and to the resurrection. The transfiguration of Jesus is witnessed by Peter, James and John, and the vision of the glorified Jesus would remain with them in darker times. Even when they know Jesus has been crucified, the memory of glory is lodged in their hearts. For us, the lesson is the same. Knowing Jesus is God and that he shares the glory of the Father can help us through dark times, confident that good will triumph in the end.

What does it say?
Jesus wants to give his disciples a vision of the glory he shares with the Father, not to impress them but to help them. They are overwhelmed and want to hang on to the moment. Moses and Elijah are with Jesus, representing the Law and the Prophets – Jesus is on equal footing with the giants of the Jewish faith. The reason for this is revealed when God speaks and calls Jesus 'Son'. No wonder the disciples are afraid. But Jesus raises them to their feet – they do not need to grovel, but to stand tall. One day, after the resurrection, they will understand the significance of what they have seen.

Main points to communicate to children
- Jesus often went away to pray with his close friends
- It is important for us also to set aside time to pray with each other
- Jesus looked like other men, but he was also God
- Jesus is God's Son
- Even the Old Testament saints recognise the importance of Jesus
- We do not need to be afraid in the presence of God
- Even when things seem dark and gloomy, God is present.

Reminder

We have the power to transfigure the lives of others by allowing our goodness to shine out. During Lent, we can ask God's help to transfigure those around us.

Teacher's Prayer

Why not say this prayer every day for the next week?

Loving Father, you live in the kingdom of light and peace.
In Jesus, you show us your love for us;
In Jesus you give us hope;
In Jesus you give us life.
Help me to follow him.
to become more like him,
and to tell others about him,
for he is Lord, for ever and ever.
Amen.

(b) Praying with Children

Penny trail

At the beginning of this week, encourage the children to save pennies throughout the duration of Lent. Ensure that the emphasis is on the penny (all children should then be able to participate). At a given time, towards the end of Lent, invite each child – one after the other – to lay their pennies on the floor, in a trail around the classroom. At the start of the trail should be a cross. (Keep the trail close to the wall, so that there is less danger of it being stepped upon!) Depending on the amount of pennies, the trail may extend to outside of the classroom. Once the trail is complete, put a picture of a needy child at the end of the trail and leave it there for the duration of the day, reminding the children that almsgiving is important when recognising the needs of others in our world. The pennies should then be collected, counted and given to Trócaire, CAFOD, SCIAF, or another charitable organisation. (This activity could be done as a whole-school event.)

Glory Cross

Have a large outline of a cross on purple frieze-paper and put this to one side. Invite the children to draw around their hand on white paper and cut it out. Children write on their paper hand, '(Name)'s *hand is a helping hand.'*

Older children can include the word, *'because ...'* and continue with an example of how they help. Younger or less able children can draw pictures of themselves being helpful. Once these are completed, a line of glue or Pritt-Stick is put at the bottom of each hand and they are placed inside the outline of the cross so that the hands flop away from the wall. The result is a large bright cross on a purple background, filled with the good deeds of the class.

Music

Using a well-known hymn such as 'Here I am, Lord', invite the children to create actions for the chorus. The whole class should learn these and when the hymn is being sung the actions can be used in the chorus. With older children, let them decide on the best movements to use. Younger children will need more direction from the teacher.

New words

Again, based on the theme of this week, invite the children to come up with new words to the well-known hymn, 'My God Loves Me'.

The precious mirror

Hang a good-sized mirror (about A4 size) on the wall at an appropriate height for the children. Write the caption, *'This person is precious to God'* (older classes) or *'God loves me'* (infants) around the mirror. This can be used during prayer but it is nice to have it in place for the duration of Lent (or even for the whole year). You will often catch a child stopping, looking in the mirror and smiling!

A variation of this is to have a box with a mirror attached inside it. Tell the children that the most important thing in the world to God is in this box. Invite them one by one to look in the box but tell them that they cannot tell anyone else in the class what they see. When they look in, they see themselves! As each child comes forward to look in the box, remind them that inside is the most important thing in the world to God.

Affirmation badges

Each child in the class is given the name of another child but they must keep it a secret. They are then given a sticker and asked to write something really positive about that person. Even though they are writing about someone else they start by writing 'I …' and continue. (For example, I am a good listener. I work hard in class. I make people laugh. I am great at football etc.) Once they have all been completed, the children write the name of the person on the back of the sticker (the bit that will be peeled off) and these are then collected by the teacher. The teacher then calls each child out and gives them their badge and reads it out to the class. The children wear their badges for the rest of the day/week.

With younger children, invite them to write, 'Kisses from God' on a sticker and cover it with kisses (xxxx). These can be worn throughout the day/week.

Affirmation letters

Each child puts his/her name at the bottom of an A4 sheet of paper. The sheets are systematically passed around the class and every child writes a positive comment about the child whose name appears on the bottom of the page. At the end, each child receives their A4 sheet of paper back with positive comments made about them. Make sure the teacher takes part too!

Hint: It is helpful to encourage the children to think of different phrases they might use before they start and to consider what they might comment upon. This will avoid them being repetitive. In addition, it is helpful to get the children to fold the top of the paper down each time they make a comment. This will mean that what they have written is covered up so the next person to comment does not copy any of the previous entries, encouraging originality.

Helping hand

Have the children seated in a circle for prayer-time. During the prayer, ask them to show you their hands. Tell them that they have to imagine that they are slowly putting on helping-hand gloves. As soon as they are on, everything that they do with their hands is good, helps others and makes God happy. Invite them to give you examples of what helping hands can do. Start them off by giving some examples of your own. Encourage the format:

'My helping hands … (e.g. make sure I am kind to others).'

Once the suggestions are made, tell the children that these imaginary gloves will remain on for the rest of the week and they have to remember all the ways they have helped while wearing them so that they can tell the others in the class at the end of the week. Finish the prayer session by saying, *'Thank you God for my helping hands'.*

Hot-seating

During an RE lesson, spend time reading, exploring and discussing the passage of the Transfiguration. Ask the children to imagine they were Peter, James or John and to write an eye-witness account of what happened that day.

During a prayer service, invite three children to sit on three seats in the middle of the floor, back to back. They become the three disciples in the passage and tell the others what they saw that day when they travelled with Jesus up the mountain. (This will be prepared and based on their written work.) The others in the class are invited to ask the two children questions about what they saw, how they felt, what they thought this meant, who they had told, what had been the reaction of others when they heard this story. This prayer activity can be finished by the whole class saying, *'Glory to God in the highest and Peace to his people on Earth'.*

Prayer

'The place on which you stand is holy ground.'
Exodus 3:1-8 (The Burning Bush)

(a)   Reminding the Teacher

Why this reading?

The Book of Genesis has at its core the story of the Creation and the Fall of humanity by the sin of Adam and Eve; when they eat of the forbidden fruit, they are banished from the garden and must live in exile. The second book of the Bible, Exodus, has at its core God's rescue of the people of Israel from slavery. By making this reading part of the Lent scriptures, the Church is pointing out that the life, death and resurrection of Jesus is the event that frees all people and opens again the gates of paradise that were closed against Adam and Eve. We see in advance the supreme importance of the events we will celebrate in Holy Week.

What does it say?

God never appears directly to people, but speaks through an angel, from a cloud, or as in this reading, from a burning bush. It is curiosity that brings Moses from his shepherding duties into the presence of God. God demands reverence from Moses – he must acknowledge God's holiness, and the holiness of the place where God speaks. God promises to rescue the people who are oppressed and to give them a place of safety, abundance and peace. And the name of God is revealed to Moses: 'I am who I am.' Jesus echoes this name repeatedly in St John's gospel when he says, 'I am the bread of life' (or light of the world etc.).

Main points to communicate to children

- God is present, even though we cannot see him
- God draws us to himself in so many different ways
- God is holy, is special, in a way we can never understand
- God hears our prayers
- God wants us to be safe and happy
- God is God for ever.

Reminder

Shrines and churches are holy places; indeed, any place can be a holy place when God is acknowledged and worshipped there.

Teacher's Prayer

Why not say this prayer every day for the next week?

God of power and might
you are holy, and your name is holy.
I approach you in reverence and awe.
Yet in spite of your greatness,
you invite me to come close to you
in the person of Jesus your Son,
my brother, my friend, my Lord.
Thank you for the gift of Jesus.
As I follow him, may he bring me
to see you face to face.
Amen.

(b) Praying with Children

Make a burning bush

Each child is given a cut-out of a flame. Ask them to colour it appropriately (front and back) and write on the flame, *'I need God because …'* or for younger children, *'God, help me to pray'*. Attach the flames to a large branch (or selection of branches tied together) to form the burning bush. This can be displayed on a wall or could be free standing, using some earth and a plant pot.

Claiming the space

The place in which prayer takes place is important. When working with children encourage them to claim the space in which they will pray. If it is in the classroom you can burn incense and place flowers in the four corners of the room. Have some peaceful music on in the background and think about effective lighting. Ask the children for ideas of how to make the room or space suitable for prayer.

Flannelling the hands

Have a bowl of water and a towel in the centre of a circle. Ask the children how they get ready when they are going somewhere special or going to meet someone they really like. Do they wash themselves or have a bath? Do they put on special clothes? What about their parents? Tell the children that today they are going to get themselves ready for meeting God in their prayer-time. One by one, invite the children to wash their hands as a way of preparing themselves for being in the presence of God.

Prayer meditation

As before, this quiet exercise brings the Word of God alive for the children. Invite them to sit calmly and have some peaceful music on in the background. Read each part of the refection and have long pauses in between, particularly if you are inviting them to imagine something. Have the children's burning bush as a focal point.

> *'Imagine that you are slowly walking up a hill. It is a beautiful day and you are really happy. You can see for miles and miles. Suddenly you hear a crackling noise and you are aware that the temperature is getting much warmer. As you walk round a bend you see an amazing sight. It is a large bush and it is on fire! The flames are high and the heat from it is so tremendous that it forces you to move back. Then you hear a voice. The voice is strong and clear and it tells you that it is God who is speaking. He says your name and you are so excited! He starts to talk to you. What does he say to you? What is he talking to you about? Listen carefully to what he is saying. Now, you start to speak to him. What do you tell him? Remember, this is God: you can tell him anything! Use this time to tell him anything you want. Listen to his response ...'* (Continue and adapt where necessary, and simplify language for infants.) Take care to gently bring the children out of the meditation at the end. Finish with: *'Glory be to the Father, and to the Son and to the Holy Spirit, Amen.'*

Prayer conversations

Ask the children to sit quietly and think of why they are special. What are they good at? What gifts do they have? Give each child a partner and tell them that they are going to tell their prayer partner what is special about themselves. Each child takes time to talk and time to listen to his/her partner. Once this has happened, invite the children to tell the rest of the class why their partner is special. They start by saying: '(Name) *is special to God because …*'

Dramatise the story

This activity works with any class in the primary school. Using a room with space (ideally an open area or gym hall) get the children to copy you as you tell the story of the burning bush. You will need to know the scripture reading well and can add to the story as you tell it. With older children why not get a group of children to recreate the story with actions. For example:

- 'One sunny day you decide to go for a long walk up a hill.' (Mime walking on the spot.)
- 'The hill is very steep and it is very difficult to climb.' (Slow down the walking.)
- 'It is a very warm day, so you decide to stop and take a drink of water.' (Rub sweat from brow and mime drinking a lot of water.)
- 'You continue to walk but suddenly you hear a strange noise up ahead.' (Put hand to ear.) The drama continues …

Pop song on theme (older classes)

Ask the children to suggest a number of well-known songs. These could be songs in the charts or popular songs that are familiar to most. Write a selection of these on the board, including one or two of your own suggestions. Tell them that in groups, they are going to select one of the songs and re-write the words using the Lenten theme of this week, 'Prayer'. Tell them that they can put actions to the song. Once these are complete, each group must sing their composition to the others in the class. Each child can vote for their favourite (but they are not allowed to vote for their own). The 'winning' song can be learned by all in the class and sung at appropriate prayer times.

Hint: Be careful in terms of song selection. If the words and tone of the original song are inappropriate then don't allow the children to use it. A variation of this is to use well-known hymns instead of pop songs.

Bring the Word alive

In groups of three ask the children to write a news report about the burning bush. One of these can be read out during a prayer service.

Forgiveness

'This man welcomes sinners and eats with them.'
Luke 15:1-3, 11-31 (The Prodigal Son)

(a)   Reminding the Teacher

Why this reading?

Lent is a time when we turn from sin and believe the Good News – a time of repentance. No parable illustrates repentance better than the Prodigal Son. This passage is rich with Lenten themes, and can inspire us to look at our lives, see where we have taken wrong turns, and motivate us to return to God. The story is accessible to children and adults alike, lends itself to dramatisation and is a rich prayer-resource. Whereas the gospel of the Transfiguration looks forward to the resurrection, this gospel looks beyond that to the eternal banquet, the great feast in the kingdom of heaven.

What does it say?

Jesus tells the story of the Prodigal Son to explain to the observant religious people around him why he spent time with outcasts and sinners. There are two sons, one short-sighted and selfish, thinking of his own pleasure, the other dutiful and sensible, remaining at home to work whilst his younger brother sought his fortune elsewhere. The father is generous and indulges his sons, but never loses hope that the younger son will see sense and return. The younger son, in the depths of his misery, has a moment of insight, sees his folly, swallows his pride and comes home. His father is waiting for him, embraces him and celebrates his return. The resentment of the older brother is swept away by the breadth of the father's love: his love is enough for both sons, with love to spare. Whichever son we may identify with, God's mercy and love overwhelm us.

Main points to communicate to children

- God loves us all equally
- Even if we turn away from God, God never abandons us
- No matter what we do, God loves us

- To return to God, we simply ask God for forgiveness
- God's generosity is amazing
- There's no need to be jealous – God's love is enough for us all.

Reminder

The story of the Prodigal Son has timeless application. It is never too late to return to the open, welcoming arms of the Father.

Teacher's Prayer

Why not say this prayer every day for the next week?

Father of forgiveness and peace
I cannot imagine your love for me,
your desire to forgive me,
your longing to welcome me home.
Let me rest in your embrace,
then warmed by your love,
show your mercy and forgiveness to others.
I ask this through Jesus Christ your Son.
Amen.

(b)   Praying with Children

Aspirations

Invite the children to sit and think about something that they have done that was wrong. Instead of telling their sin, invite them to share with the rest of the class what they will try hard to do. Give them an example by being a witness to your own faith. Tell them something that you have done wrong and explain to them how you can turn this into something positive to ask God for. For example, a teacher may tell the class that he/she is sorry for arguing with his/her friend. The prayer is then offered: *'Dear God, I will try hard to be kind.'*

One-line dramas

Pick one of the themes from the reading – for example, 'God loves us all equally'. Devise a simple drama that illustrates the point. You could have five children in a row, one of whom has no shoes on. A 'dignitary' comes along, shakes the hands of each, pauses in front of the one with no shoes, looks at the feet, gives a look of disgust, does not shake hands, then moves on to the others. A 'Jesus' figure comes along, looks at each person intently, shakes every hand alike. The message of the drama can be reinforced in a prayer, chant or some other way.

Mending what is broken

Have a large paper jigsaw of a heart on the floor or on the wall. (This can be easily made by drawing a large heart on some paper or card and cutting it up into five or so pieces.) As a child comes forward and takes a piece of the heart away, the class repeat the phrase, *'Sin breaks'*. Invite another child to take a second piece of the jigsaw away and the phrase is said once more. Continue doing this until only one piece of the heart remains.

Read the story of the Prodigal Son to the children

After the story, invite each child with the jigsaw piece to put it back in the correct place. As each child does this the rest of the class repeat the phrase, *'Forgiveness makes'*. Finish with the class praying the 'Our Father' together.

Tasting reflection – with actions (infants)

Ask the children to imagine that they are tasting something very sour. They mime putting it into their mouth and it is horrible! It makes their eyes water. It makes them shiver! It makes them suck in their cheeks. Ask them to show you horrible disapproving faces. Quickly they swallow it in one big gulp to make it go away! Now they imagine tasting a lovely piece of chocolate. This melts on their tongue and tingles every part of their mouth with sweetness. It is delicious! They lick their lips because it is so wonderful. Slowly they swallow it and they close their eyes as it slips down their throat. The taste is so wonderful they don't want it to go away.

Tell the children that when we try to live without God, it just isn't nice, it's like the sour taste. When we know God's love for us, we know it is so sweet, it is so wonderful.

Sin bin

Ask the children to write down their sins on a piece of paper and put it in an envelope. During a prayer service, with reflective music on in the background, encourage the children to hold the envelope in their hands and to think carefully about what they have written. Invite them to speak to God in their own hearts and to tell him that they are sorry. The teacher passes round a basket and tells the children to place the envelope in the basket. Reassure the children that the envelopes will never be opened. If possible, have a fire burning in the playground (management permission and appropriate supervision are essential). From a safe distance, the children watch you empty the contents of the basket onto the fire. As the envelopes burn, the children can sing, *'Be still and know that I am God'*.

Sorry beads

A long piece of string is passed around a class of children seated in a circle. Each child takes the string and ties a knot in it (if the children are too young, get each child to thread a bead onto the string). Each knot or bead shows they are sorry for something. As they tie the knot or thread the bead, get them to say, *'I am sorry, God'*. When all the knots/beads are in place, the teacher ties the ends together and forms *Sorry Beads*. These can be placed somewhere on the classroom altar and used during a prayer session in Lent. The teacher can hold the beads and point to each one as the children repeat a suitable phrase, e.g. 'God forgives me'.

'Open your hand and forgive'

Children are asked to sit in a circle with their left hand clenched. The teacher explains how a closed hand is cold and does not represent forgiveness. The teacher says to the first child, *'Open your hand and forgive'* whilst opening the child's hand. The child then turns to the next person, opens their hand whilst saying the same thing. When all hands are open the children join hands and repeat a forgiveness prayer recited by the teacher. (Make up your own or say the children's familiar act of contrition, even for classes that haven't made the Sacrament of Reconciliation.)

Forgiveness chorus

Each child repeatedly sings (prompted by teacher) *'I am sorry'* and they have to sing it on a different note from the other children, creating a babble of noise! This starts quietly and when the teacher raises a hand the noise should increase. When the hand is lowered, the singing gets softer. When the teacher claps hands the children stop and the teacher sings, *'I forgive you'* and the children respond by singing *'I forgive you'* three times, on the same note as the teacher.

Limerick

In groups of four, ask the children to come up with a Limerick or poem based on 'The Prodigal Son'. Here is an example of a first verse:

Two brothers they had a rich dad
One of them was very bad
He took his dad's money
He thought this was funny
He left home but then he was sad.

New Life

'I am the resurrection and the life.'
John 11:25 (Lazarus)

(a) Reminding the Teacher

Why this reading?

The week before Palm (Passion) Sunday when the whole drama of the trial, sentencing, suffering and death of Jesus is proclaimed in our churches, the gospel of the raising of Lazarus is read. It spells out in advance the significance of the resurrection of Jesus – the power of God is stronger than death, our greatest enemy. Jesus himself is the key to eternal life. Having heard the account of the raising of Lazarus, we can accept in faith the rising of Jesus from the dead, and his promise to us that we will live for ever.

What does it say?

The raising of Lazarus is significant for us all. In the gospel account, we learn that Jesus can suffer the pain of loss, and grieve as we do. However, Jesus can see beyond his grief to the point where he can prophesy that even sickness can bring glory to God. Martha believes in resurrection in a general sense, but Jesus teaches something new: he himself is the resurrection and the life. Friendship with Jesus raises us to life, everlasting life. In his grief Jesus opens his heart to his Father, and prays that the miracle he is about to work will bring people to faith. The command of Jesus, 'Lazarus, here, come out' was effective beyond the barrier of death – and Lazarus rose. 'Unbind him, let him go free' again expresses the desire of Jesus to free us from all that prevents us from truly living.

Main points to communicate to children

- Jesus loves his friends
- Even when his friend died, Jesus did not lose hope
- Jesus knows our sadness and wants to comfort us
- Jesus helps us to live, first on earth, then in heaven

- We believe that Jesus looks after those who have died
- Jesus wants us to be free of anything that might harm us.

Reminder

We believe that Jesus lived and died – this is an act of belief. We believe that Jesus rose again – this is an act of faith.

When we believe in the resurrection, we associate ourselves with it, and find life.

Teacher's Prayer

Why not say this prayer every day for the next week:

Heavenly Father,
you know all my sorrows and my joys
my hopes and my fears.
Help me to remember
that Jesus your Son
conquered death;
strengthen my faith in his resurrection
so I may live in hope,
bring hope to others
and share in eternal life.
I ask this through Christ the Lord.
Amen.

(b)   Praying with Children

New Life classroom diary

Have a classroom 'New Life' diary. This can be made very simply from stapling some A3 paper together and decorating the front page. Ask the children to be conscious of any new life that they see and give them the opportunity each day during prayer to tell you about it. This could be from buds on a tree to new babies to new cars (all signs of growth and development). Record their entries in the New Life diary and have it on display, and available for all to see.

'You Raise Me Up' (older classes)

Print out the words of the popular song, 'You Raise Me Up' (obtainable online; take note of any copyright conditions).

In groups of five, ask the children to put actions to the words and to learn these together as a group. Each group shows the others in the class. The version considered best by the class has to be learned by all and used during a prayer session/assembly. (Other popular songs/hymns can be used too.)

(Mustard and) Cress seed cross

At the beginning of the week, get each group of children to plant some mustard and/or cress seeds in a tray of potting compost or earth, in the shape of a cross. Water this. In a matter of days, the cress will grow and the result will be crosses full of growth and life. Make the connection with the children that Lent and Easter are a time of growth and new life.

Happy cross

During classroom prayer, cover a cross in bright shiny resurrection foil; make reference in prayer to the cross not just being about sadness but pointing to future happiness.

Wall crosses: Death and Resurrection

Draw around two children, one with arms outstretched, the other with arms raised up. Arrange the children in a circle and have the two outlines on the floor. Give each child a small square piece of paper with 'Lord, you don't like …' written on it. Ask the children to quietly write down some bad things in their life or in the world (for example, poverty, selfishness, killing, unhappiness, bullying, bad words etc.). One by one the children stick the pieces of paper inside the first outline. Give them a second piece of paper, all different colours, with 'Lord, you love …' written on it and invite the class to write about hopeful things and the goodness in their world (for example, forgiveness, love, happiness, laughter, smiling, kindness). Again, the children stick their messages inside the second image with the raised arms. The two outlines can be displayed.

Finish by singing a hymn together or saying a prayer.

'Why worry?' collage

The gospel passage reminds us that there will be sunshine after the rain. Instead of worrying, we should trust in God. Prepare three large pieces of paper (landscape) in the following way. On the first, glue cotton wool balls in a straight line, right across the middle of the paper. On the second piece do the same except leave some gaps in the line of cotton wool. Leave the third one blank. Put the children into three groups.

1)   The first make a collage (using colours/images from magazines) illustrating a gloomy day. The cotton wool represents clouds and so above the clouds is sun and a blue sky, but below is gloomy and dark.

2)   The second group take the picture with the broken clouds. They make a collage, but this time the sun is beaming through the breaks in the cloud.

3)   The last group make a collage of a bright and sunny day!

Each collage will display a caption. The first should read, *'Trust in God even when you are sad'*. The second, *'Look for signs of God's Love'*. And the third, *'Be happy because God is always with us'*. Once finished, the three collages can be used in prayer.

Seed meditation (Infants)

Have reflective music on in the background. Tell the children to find a space in the room/hall. Tell them to curl up on their feet, into a ball and to imagine that they are little seeds in the cold earth. God's love invites them to grow, so they begin to slowly grow and unfurl. As they get taller they reach up towards God. When they have reached their full growth they are tall and long and stretched right up to God. (Add to and adapt where necessary.)

Say a prayer together when they're stretched.

New Life Litany

Invite the children to write their own litanies. Based on the story of Lazarus, the children (in small groups, even pairs) write a list of things that Jesus does. They should aim for between six and ten. They then write a one-line response, asking for something from Jesus, again linked to the story. As each line of the list or 'litany' is read, the rest of the class repeat the response. Here is an example:

You show love to others
　　Jesus, strengthen our faith
You teach the Good News
　　Jesus, strengthen our faith
You comfort the mourning
　　Jesus, strengthen our faith
You give hope to the weak
　　Jesus, strengthen our faith
You raise us to new life
　　Jesus, strengthen our faith
You pray for us to your Father
　　Jesus, strengthen our faith.
(The litany continues …)

Why not use a different litany every morning for a week instead of/in addition to the normal classroom prayer.

Hosanna!

'Blessings on the king who comes, in the name of the Lord.'
Luke 19:28-40 (Palm Sunday)

(a)   Reminding the Teacher

Why this reading?

During the Easter Triduum (Holy Thursday, Good Friday and Easter Sunday) the Church celebrates different aspects of the saving work of Jesus Christ. At the beginning of Holy Week, we commemorate the beginning of this final act in the drama of the earthly life of Jesus – his entry into Jerusalem, being greeted by the people as a king. He will be crucified, with the description 'Jesus of Nazareth, King of the Jews' nailed to his cross. And we now know him as the risen, triumphant king of heaven and earth. This reading reminds us of who Jesus is, why he came and what he achieves for us and for all people.

What does it say?

The entrance of Jesus into Jerusalem is, like the events that follow, fulfilment of Old Testament prophecy. Who Jesus is and what Jesus does has been foretold and is part of God's plan for the salvation of humankind. Even in simple events such as the entry of Jesus into the holy city, the disciples can rejoice that God is acting powerfully in their midst. In fact the disciples are not simply shouting out in praise of God, they are proclaiming the coming of the King and announcing that the kingdom of peace and glory is at hand. Nature itself would cry out if the disciples kept silence, such is the importance of the coming of the Lord to Jerusalem.

Main points to communicate to children

- Jesus is a king, but not like other kings
- Everything Jesus does is part of God's plan
- When we see what God does, we want to shout out in praise
- Jesus brings peace
- Jesus is the most important person in the world
- We welcome Jesus just like the crowds welcomed him.

Reminder

In Lent we celebrate what has already happened, as in the entry of Jesus into Jerusalem; at the same time, Lent looks forward to the resurrection, and to the return of Christ in glory. So Lent is austere, tinged with celebration.

Teacher's Prayer

Why not say this prayer every day for the next week?

Merciful God, you have given us Jesus Christ;
he is the perfect example of love, of service and of sacrifice.
As by grace we share his life, may we also share his glory
in the kingdom where he lives and reigns with you and the Holy Spirit,
One God, world without end.
Amen.

(b)   Praying with Children

Make a palm tree

Cut out palm leaves (long, thin leaves) and give two to each child to colour in. When the leaves are ready, bind the base of each leaf to a trunk (broom handle, kitchen foil roll etc.) with string or wool, but keep the leaves moving up the pole. Stand the pole upright, and then bend the upper part of the leaves outwards. This can be the visual focus for the week.

On the last day of the week, have a prayer focused around palms. Each child removes a leaf and holds it during prayer. At various points during prayer, sing the chorus of 'Give me joy in my heart' which is,

Sing 'Hosanna!'
Sing 'Hosanna!'
Sing 'Hosanna!' to the King of Kings (x2)

Each time the chorus is sung the children wave their palm.

Chanting litany

Create a litany with the class (using the same format that is in the last chapter). This time the response repeated after each line is *'Hosanna, Hosanna, Hosanna!'* and should be sung. A very simple way to sing it is to sing the first *Hosanna* on a note, go to a higher note for the second Hosanna and again for the third.

God bless you

During prayer, each child is invited to bless his/her neighbour with the sign of the cross on their forehead, saying 'God bless you'.

Narrative-led drama

Make space in the classroom for the drama. Tell the children that they have to follow the teacher's directions. Tell them they are going about their daily business, doing their shopping, chatting, playing with their friends. Someone far away has shouted that Jesus is coming so start looking around for Jesus. Look for him everywhere. Point to him coming in the distance. Tell the children to get their palms (have them ready). Make two lines in the room leading to a cross. Jesus walks through waving. They wave their palms. He reaches the cross. All kneel and pray in silence.

Litany of Hosanna

This is a very simple litany for use in any stage in the primary school! Each child says, '*Jesus,* (name) *welcomes you!*' All shout 'Hosanna!' x 3.

Jesus as King of Love

Each child makes a small crown (kingship) and a heart (love). During prayer, these are placed in front of an icon or picture of Jesus. As they are placed each child says, '*Hosanna, Jesus*'.

With older children, ask them to write a message to Jesus on one of the images, praising and thanking him for being the King of Love.

Guided meditation

This meditation welcomes Jesus into the children's hearts. Using the format of the meditations in the previous chapters create your own, incorporating the following main points:

1. Be calm
2. Say 'sorry' in your heart
3. Think of what you need
4. Think of how much Jesus loves you
5. Finish with, *'Now just welcome him in your heart'*.

End with a prayer or well-known hymn.

Themes (See page 53)

- God is *our* Father – we are a community
- God is our *Father* – a loving parent
- God lives in heaven
- May your name be held holy – we should praise God
- Your kingdom come – God is king of heaven and earth
- Your will be done – God's way should be our way
- Give us today – we are to ask God for what we need
- Our daily bread – we need God like we need food
- God forgives
- We need to ask for forgiveness
- It is important we forgive others
- Do not put us to the test – keep us strong
- God protects us from harm.

Chapter 4
Pray for us – Celebrating Mary and the Saints: *foundations, ideas and resources*

Teachers' background knowledge – Mary and the Saints

Mary and the Saints are important to Catholic worship and prayer. We believe that they are in heaven, in the presence of God. We believe too that they are concerned with the world, praying for us before the Lord. We ask them to pray with us and for us, and believe that they help us. We use Saints (with a capital 'S') to denote the holy women and men who have been canonised (officially declared as such by the Church), and saints (with a small 's') to denote women and men of holy lives, whom we believe to be in heaven, but about whom the Church has made no official pronouncement. Traditional terminology speaks of the Church here on earth as the 'Church militant' and the Saints in heaven as the 'Church Triumphant'. The reality is that we are one in communion with them; our communion is imperfect, theirs is perfect. There are a number of approaches to praying with the Saints that can be taken with children; the exercises suggested fall into one of these categories:

- Mary and the Saints are part of our family in heaven
- We pray for each other in this life, and we don't stop when we get to heaven
- We celebrate the feasts of Mary and the Saints like we celebrate birthdays
- We can celebrate the 'Name-Days' of children (the feast day of a Saint with whom the child shares a name)
- We can plan classroom prayer or assemblies focusing on a virtue – courage for example – and illustrate the theme with the life of a Saint
- Celebrating Saints can be inspirational and motivational for children: Saints are people we want to imitate.

Some acknowledgement needs to be made that there are stories about Saints – especially ancient Saints – that might not be strictly historical: St George and the dragon, for example.

Colours associated with Mary and the Saints

Traditionally, Mary is associated with the colour blue; different shades of blue are represented in the appearances, icons, paintings and statues of Our Lady, but the colour blue is a constant.

Martyrs are generally associated with the colour red, signifying the blood they shed for their faith. Apostles also are associated with red: like martyrs, it is generally 'blood red', or a darker shade.

All other Saints are associated with white, like the saints gathered round the throne of the lamb in the Book of Revelation. It is the colour of purity, and the colour associated with the transfigured Christ.

Symbols associated with Mary and the Saints

Mary is sometimes depicted standing, sometimes sitting on a throne; often she wears a crown, a sign that she is Queen of heaven. Usually (apart from popular depictions such as Our Lady of Lourdes), she is carrying the Christ-child – her first title is 'Mother of God'. Sometimes Mary is depicted with a corona of twelve stars around her head, where she is seen as representing the Church, with reference to John's vision in the Book of Revelation. Again, she is sometimes shown crushing a serpent under her feet, an allusion to the prophecy of Isaiah. On icons of Mary, she is depicted against a gold background, symbolising heaven. Icons always name the people depicted in them. Mary is always described as Mother of God – always designated in association with her Divine Son.

St Joseph carries a lily, a sign of his purity. St Peter carries keys, an allusion to the power to bind and loose given to him by Jesus. St Patrick usually carries a shamrock, which he used to teach the mystery of the Trinity. St Andrew carries the distinctive saltire cross (X-shaped), referring to the manner of his execution. St George is usually on horseback, carrying a spear and slaying the dragon – a warrior Saint.

All these symbols may be used in classroom prayer or assemblies, providing a visual, creative focus for children.

National and Devotional associations

Traditionally, every country has a Patron Saint, whose day is celebrated each year. The Saint concerned is usually associated with the country historically, but not always. And there is a Patron Saint for just about everything in life: travelling (St

Christopher), childbirth (St Gerard Majella), horse racing (St Non, the mother of St David of Wales), lost items (St Anthony of Padua) and lost causes (St Jude), to name but a few.

How we pray to Mary and the Saints

Asking Mary and the Saints to pray with us and for us is never a substitute for praying directly to God; rather, they are part of the Church, the body, which has Christ as its head. We pray to God, asking, thanking and praising. And we ask the Saints to join us. Sometimes, at special moments, we join in their prayer; for example, the first part of the Eucharistic Prayer at Mass is called the 'Preface'. It always concludes with a variation on the lines: '… and now, we join the angels and saints in their unending hymn of praise as we say, *"Holy, Holy, Holy, Lord God of power and might"*.'

We ask Mary and the Saints to pray for us to God; a litany addressing Mary or the Saints usually has the response, 'Pray for us'. The Hail Mary, the best known prayer to Our Lady, concludes, 'Pray for us now and at the hour of our death. Amen'.

Mary and the Nations

Mary the Mother of God is truly an international figure. Continents, countries, regions, cities, towns and villages often have their own devotional image of Mary. She can be depicted as African, Chinese, European, or whatever the nationality of the people who have devotion to her. This presents an opportunity for school situations where children from different ethnic backgrounds are present: a way of celebrating cultural diversity in the context of the unity of the faith.

Traditional devotion

There is a rich treasury of liturgical (official) and devotional (more informal) prayer with regard to Mary and the Saints. The prayers from the Mass and the Divine Office (the official prayer of the Church, the main parts of which are Morning, Evening and Night Prayer) are an invaluable resource, which with a little interpretation can be adapted for use with children, or used for themes associated with the Saints. In addition, with regard to Mary, there is a wealth of tradition, including the Mysteries of the Rosary, the Hail Mary, Magnificat, Litanies and other prayers. It's always important to acquaint children with the tradition, and important too to help them pray individually and creatively; this way they will have the best of both worlds – familiar with the tradition, and with a deeper understanding of what it means.

Mary, and how we can think of her:
> *Mary as the mother of Jesus*
> *Mary as our mother*
> *Mary the compassionate one*
> *Mary of my country*
> *Mary who cares*
> *Mary, Constant Helper*
> *Mary of Our School.*

The Saints, and how we can think of them:
> *Saints who give everything*
> *Saints with inspiring lives*
> *Saints who are special patrons (of our school, of the sick etc.)*
> *Saints who have changed history*
> *Ordinary Saints with extraordinary lives*
> *Saints for times of crisis*
> *Praying the virtues of the Saints.*

An example of a structure of a classroom prayer or assembly focusing on Mary and the Saints

Bringing the class together

As with other prayer experiences, we begin by bringing people together: a song, hymn or chant unites the children and sets the tone for the prayer which follows. At the end of the section, there are suggestions for hymns, scripture readings and other resources for celebrating Mary and the Saints.

Invoking Mary or the Saint on whom the prayer is focused

This could be an introduction explaining what the prayer is to be about, and why Mary or a particular Saint is being featured. It could take the form of a drama, a dramatic tableau, a news report. A variety of ways of presenting a theme are suggested earlier in this book (see pages 52, 53 and 54).

The Word

As in all our classroom and assembly prayer, the Word of God is at its heart. This may take the form of a reading or even a single line from the scriptures. The feast day readings of Our Lady (Mary) and the Saints are rich resources here.

Developing the theme

The presentation of the Word may be followed by a paraphrase, which brings out the meaning of the text. Again, there are many examples elsewhere in this book of how to develop and go more deeply into the theme you and the children have chosen.

The prayer

This is where we ask Mary or the particular Saint for their help. It can be a prayer the children have written; a Litany written with the children is often a creative approach here, and is often easy to develop. For example, encourage the children to describe St Joseph. He must have been kind, trusting, patient, caring, full of love for Mary and Jesus; being a carpenter, he must have worked hard, taught the child Jesus family values. So a litany to St Joseph could take the following form:

> *St Joseph, you are kind*
>> *Pray for us*
> *St Joseph, you are trusting*
>> *Pray for us*
> *St Joseph, you are patient*
>> *Pray for us*
> *St Joseph, you cared for your family*
>> *Pray for us*
> *St Joseph, you are full of love*
>> *Pray for us*
> *St Joseph, you worked hard*
>> *Pray for us*
> *St Joseph, you are now in heaven*
>> *Pray for us.*

It's as easy as that! Children may then be invited to present particular petitions to St Joseph, and round off these petitions with a prayer they have created.

All prayer to Mary and the Saints is asking them to pray to God for us, so it is appropriate to close by addressing God, Father, Son or Spirit, directly.

Closing the prayer

A blessing, prepared by the children may be used; the Sign of the Cross may be made. A blessing can round off the prayer experience. And a final hymn, song or chant brings the worship to conclusion.

As with other classroom and assembly prayer we have explored, we need to consider the following:

Claiming the space: visual, symbolic decoration of the classroom or hall, providing a focus; music playing as children enter or leave, or for a minute or so before prayer begins. Candles, incense, statues or icons can all be used to good effect.

Balance: The overall balance of the prayer between music, word, visual focus, symbolic action, song, appeal to other senses. And also balance between subsequent prayer experiences: one might be more visual, another more musical, etc.

Theme: This can come from the life or characteristics of the Saint, a particular virtue, the need for which the Saint's help is being asked. Unlike the other sections of this book, scripture passages are more likely to be chosen to fit in with the theme already decided, as to begin with scripture, decide a theme and then try to fit in the Saint would be too contrived.

Process

Tapping into the children's creativity is, as always, the key. To have the children involved at every stage of producing the classroom prayer or assembly is vital, and is more important than attaining a polished result without children being involved creatively. Creating liturgy is engaging, educating, catechising and results in prayer that children will take both ownership of and understand.

Prayer ideas and resources

(These should be read in conjunction with the other sections of this book, which will suggest a number of further ideas and resources. Those below are simply suggestions to help you and the class get started.)

1. The family of God

With the children, create a display with photos, drawings or name-cards of their immediate family members. Then add pictures, drawings or name-cards of Mary or the particular Saint who is to be the focus of the prayer time.

2. Praying with beads

Use rosary beads to pray the Saints: write up the name of fifty Saints; say on the first of the ten beads, *Saint Paul (for example), pray for us.* On the second bead, *St Mark, pray for us*; on the third bead, *St Margaret, pray for us*; and so on. On the beads in between the different decades, pray the Hail Mary. This prayer exercise could be a devotion in itself, or form part of a longer classroom/assembly prayer exercise.

3. Daily petitions

Introduce a certain Saint by showing a picture or icon; speak about the Saint's life or a particular virtue shown by the Saint, or about what the Saint is patron of. Invite the children to compose a petition to the Saint, asking for prayers for their intention. These petitions are then placed before the picture or statue for the day.

4. Living like a Saint
Choose a particular Saint for the week. With the children, discuss five good points about that Saint, and allocate one for each day of the school week. Each child is asked to try and live that virtue or characteristic for the day, before moving onto the next one the following day. Encourage feedback, either in conversation or in a prayer diary (older children) as to how they succeeded each day.

5. If I were a Saint
Invite the children to write or talk about which Saint they would like to be. What good things would they do? Who would they most like to help? Use their ideas or compositions in classroom/assembly prayer.

6. Making medals
Using clay or other modelling materials, the children can make medals in honour of Mary or one of the Saints. On one side of the medal can be the symbol of the Saint (keys for St Peter, for example). On the other side a cross or other symbol of Christ. These medals may be used to decorate a shrine in the classroom, or children can hold them (or wear them) whilst praying.

7. Saints that we know
St Paul refers to all Christians as saints (literally meaning 'holy ones'). There are many people around us who are saints in this sense: people who care for others, people who are inspiring, people who live heroic lives, people who pray for others constantly, people who are entirely selfless. Invite the children to think of someone they could call a saint, and to describe that person and say why they admire them so much; they might choose a family member or relative, a teacher or someone else they look up to. In classroom prayer, use the examples they have given to inspire the children to live like the people they admire.

8. Flying the flag
Work with the children on making a flag to celebrate the patron of the school or local parish. This flag can be used indoors or outdoors, to mark special occasions. Paint the symbol of the saint, write the name of the saint, copy an image of the saint – whatever will help the prayer and celebration.

Chapter 5
God and Me! – Personal Prayer with Children: *creative ideas for individual prayer*

Introduction

This chapter is slightly different from the other chapters in that it supports teachers in exploring creative ways to develop *personal* prayer for children. Our previous three chapters have focused on praying together in class and at assembly during the liturgical seasons of Advent and Lent. Chapter 5 is different in that it focuses on *individual* prayer and can be used at any other time during the school or liturgical year. It is appropriate for classroom and individual use, and can be adapted for a variety of situations.

Prayer can never fully be taught. It is much more than technique, much more than simply asking for what we need; it is a conversation with God, not merely of words, but of heart, mind, body and soul. This may sound daunting, but it needn't be! In this chapter we offer thirty exercises to encourage children – and you, the teacher – to communicate effectively with God. We recommend that individual prayer exercises are promoted a week at a time, so that children will become familiar with them before moving on to the next. With so many suggestions, and in addition to the Advent and Lent packs, this means that children will have the opportunity for personal prayer every day of the school year.

Each exercise is different from the others; some are more fully developed with background explanations and therefore are suitable for adaptation to various different situations. Others are simple, self-explanatory exercises. The theme index, found in the contents list, suggests appropriate exercises for different occasions.

Teaching from experience

We highly recommend that you, the teacher, try each prayer exercise yourself before introducing it to children. You will have a clearer idea of what to expect, and will be in a better position to adapt the exercises as appropriate.

Length of prayer exercise

There is no right or wrong length of time for personal prayer, but a general guideline would be to keep the prayer sufficiently short so that the children will not get restless, but long enough for the experience to be meaningful. With children unused to personal prayer, three minutes may be long enough; as children become more accustomed to personal prayer, five, seven or even ten minutes may be appropriate. It helps to say beforehand how long the exercise is going to last.

Journaling

Older children may benefit from keeping a personal journal or prayer diary. They can be encouraged to make a brief note on each prayer exercise undertaken. The entry may be simple: name the exercise undertaken (e.g. Jesus Prayer), where undertaken (e.g. classroom), whether alone or with others, how long the exercise lasted, how they felt (e.g. calm), what they prayed for and any other points of note.

Prayer Exercises

The Jesus Prayer (Forgiveness; Contemplation)

This prayer exercise is one of the most ancient in the Christian tradition, and also one of the easiest. It has a variety of forms, one of which we will explore here, and others in different prayer exercises. It is a prayer of repetition, invoking the name of Jesus. The purpose of the prayer is not the name itself, but the way it leads the person praying into a reflective, prayerful conversation with God.

Pray

There is little preparation required with this form of prayer; the exercise is suitable for when you are sitting still, walking or working. You might wish to mark the beginning and end of the prayer exercise with the Sign of the Cross.

Until you are used to this form of prayer, begin by saying the name 'Jesus' out loud, pausing for a moment, saying it again, and so on. After a minute, simply repeat the name silently, keeping the slow, measured pace. That's it.

You might wish to discuss with the class how the exercise went, what the experience was like for individual children. There is no right or wrong experience. If the children report being distracted, remind them simply to come back to the name again and again.

At home

No adaptation is required to do this prayer exercise at home.

Candle Prayer (Contemplation; Guidance)

Candles have been used in Christian prayer throughout history, to provide light, but also to symbolise the presence of Jesus, 'the Light of the World' (*CCC* 2466), to decorate prayer-space and to provide an effective visual focus for personal prayer. This prayer exercise is a form of contemplation (we will be exploring other forms later).

The use of candles in any environment must be carefully supervised, with special emphasis on safety. The candle should be in a place where it is easily visible to all, and placed on a suitable fire-resistant surface, or in a fire-resistant dish.

Pray

The exercise begins with the Sign of the Cross, made slowly and prayerfully. The person praying may start off by saying silently, 'Lord, let your light shine in my heart'. After that, the person praying simply looks at the candle flame; no words are necessary, no special efforts to direct thoughts in any direction are needed. The contemplation of the candle flame is in the context of the opening prayer, and the time of prayer can be brought to a close with the words, 'Lord, let me bring your light to others' (this may be spoken out loud by the teacher in a classroom situation) and the Sign of the Cross.

This prayer exercise may be followed by a brief discussion on how we can be light to others, bringing hope and peace. Each child may be invited to choose one way of being light to others for the rest of that day, or the whole of the week.

At home

The preparation and lighting of the candle at home should be overseen by a responsible adult, who will also supervise the entire prayer session. The emphasis at all times must be on safety.

Asking Prayer (Petition)

There are three traditional types of prayer. These are intercession, thanksgiving and praise. This is a version of prayer of intercession (we will use variations of this approach later). When we pray this type of prayer, we remind ourselves of our dependence on God, that God loves us and cares for us, and that no prayer goes unheard. We tend to pray this type of prayer most often, aware of our own needs and the needs of others. It is good to remind ourselves from time to time to give thanks to God and to praise God too.

Pray

Each child writes down or illustrates any intentions they have. They can be guided by suggesting categories of prayer: family, self, those in need, friends, events. After the Sign of the Cross is made together, the children quietly choose an intention from their list, close their eyes, and chat silently with God about that intention; this can be with few words or many. They then just sit still for a few seconds (up to a minute, say), then choose another intention from their list and repeat the process. The time of prayer is brought to a close with the teacher saying a prayer out loud. This could simply be a sentence: 'Dear God, you love us and you care for us; please hear all our prayers. Amen.'

Pencils and paper are provided for each child. Categories of intentions may be displayed on the board for children to refer back to when they are composing their list. A variation on this prayer exercise would be to focus on a different category of prayer each day of the school week.

Discussion may follow this exercise, so children become aware of the concerns and intentions of each other. If important intentions (for example, the illness of a family member) are expressed, the teacher may suggest that each child add this intention to their own list the following day.

A letter to God (Conversation with God)

This prayer involves each child (and the teacher, of course) writing a letter to God. It is sometimes easier to express important things by writing them down. This also helps us to put our thoughts in order, and in a way we can come back to at a later time. Letters play an important part in the New Testament, teaching the Christian faith, telling us about the life of the early Church and the first Christians.

Pray

Each child writes a letter; it can be addressed to God (the Father), to Jesus, or to the Holy Spirit, as the teacher or child thinks appropriate. The content of the letter can be left up to the imagination of the child – or the teacher may suggest a theme, or a number of topics the child might address. The style of the letter may be chatty, informal, as though to a friend. Depending on the time available, the letter may be brief or longer. A letter could be started on the first day of the week, and added to each successive day. When the letter (or section of the letter) is finished, the writer sits with it, reads it slowly, imagining God reading it. The teacher brings the prayer exercise to a close by saying a short prayer out loud: 'Dear God, thank you for being with me every day. Thank you for loving me. Amen.'

Pencil and paper should be provided for each child. The teacher may write up topics that may be covered in the letters and, where appropriate, help children in the writing of the letter. After the prayer exercise, the teacher may invite children to read out what they have written that day (preferably after the teacher has seen the letter and ensured it is appropriate) for public reading.

At home

An adult may take the role of teacher when this prayer exercise is undertaken at home. Topics can be suggested for the letter, or a simple template produced, dividing the letter into sections; for example, where the writer is, how he or she is feeling, what the weather is like, what they want to ask God for, what they want to say 'thank you' for.

Rosary (Mary)

This is an adaptation of the traditional Catholic devotion, prayed with the help of beads. The beads are usually in five sets of ten beads, each preceded by a single bead. This prayer exercise is repetitive, and helps reinforce the chosen focus. The use of beads can help the child to concentrate in situations where it might otherwise be difficult (where there is background noise, for example). The exercise is suitable for a variety of situations, not just for classroom or home. It is not a substitute for praying the rosary in the traditional manner, which should also be encouraged in the Catholic primary school (see another variation of this on page 103: adapting the tradition Rosary).

Pray

The exercise begins with the Sign of the Cross, made, as always, slowly and reverently. Holding the first single bead between thumb and forefinger, the child says, 'Jesus, I love you'. Then on each of the ten beads that follow the child says silently, 'Mary, help me to love Jesus more and more'. This pattern is repeated until all five decades (sets of ten beads) have been prayed, or for as long as time allows. The teacher brings the time of prayer to a close by leading children in the Hail Mary. This prayer may be adapted, with the individual beads focusing on God the Father, and the decade beads on Jesus, for example. Also, the intention of the prayer can change day by day: 'Jesus, I want to be like you' and 'Mary, help me to be like your Son'.

The intention of the prayer for each day may be displayed on the board. If children do not have rosary beads, they can make them by knotting string and tying the ends; or by using cord and beads as supplied in craft shops, separating the beads by knotting the cord.

After the prayer exercise, children may be led in discussion as to how their prayer might be answered: 'How can I love Jesus more?' and 'How can I be more like Jesus'.

Praising Prayer (Praise)

This method of prayer was practised by the first monks in the Sinai desert in the fourth century AD, and has remained part of the Church's tradition. It can be seen at Mass every day, and is suitable for personal prayer. It is a prayer of mind, body and spirit.

Pray

Lead a discussion with children about how good God is, and what great things God does. Remark on how good it is when we receive praise for what we've done, so it is only right that we praise God for all that God has done.

Invite the children to stand, to think of how great and wonderful God is, and to raise their arms up towards heaven. Keep the position for a minute or so, or until the arms tire, then lower the arms. Repeat the exercise two or three times, each time praising God with arms raised to heaven.

You can invite the children to share how they feel after this kind of prayer. It is not unusual for them to feel uplifted.

At home

No adaptation is required to do this prayer exercise at home.

Sunbathe Prayer (Praise)

The Psalms – the hymns of God's Chosen people adopted by the Christian Church for its worship – suggest many different forms of prayer because they have been part of the worship of God for thousands of years. One of the Psalms says, 'Let the light of your face shine upon us, O Lord, and we shall be saved'. This sentiment is rooted in the Jewish and Christian belief that we depend on God for life, and in God's presence, we find life.

All growing things depend on the sun. Plants change the sun's rays into energy that enables them to flourish. Without these plants, there would be no food chain, no animal life – and no human life. Sunshine is a great symbol of the life God gives, and offers a model of prayer.

Pray

Explain this in suitable words to children, and invite them to sit still, facing a cross or icon or symbol representing God, with their eyes closed. Tell them to imagine God looking at them, smiling on them, warming them with pure love. As God looks at them in this way, they are receiving God's light and are enabled to grow. God's gaze is always good, nothing to be afraid of, something to be sought. Gradually, the length of this exercise may be increased as children become used to the idea of 'sun-bathing' in God's gaze.

Bring the prayer session to an end with an appropriate prayer, concluding, perhaps, by adapting words from the Psalm: *Thank you Lord for shedding the light of your face upon us; thank you for the warmth of your love. Thank you for giving us life. Let us always live in the light of your face. Amen.*

At home

No adaptation is required to do this prayer exercise at home.

Heaven Opening Prayer (Holy Communion; Praise; Saints; Angels)

Each time the priest says the Preface at Mass (the opening part of the Eucharistic Prayer), it finishes in a similar way, for example, 'And with all the angels and saints, we join in their unending hymn of praise as we say, '*Holy, holy, holy, God of power and might …*' This is a beautiful acknowledgment of the spiritual reality of the Mass: heaven is opened up, and we on earth glimpse the glory, and are invited to join in the eternal hymn of praise that is forever being offered before God.

This may be explained simply to the children – that when we pray, the heavens are opened and we are very close to the angels and saints; and that they pray with us all the time.

Pray

Invite the children to look upwards, and to close their eyes. Describe briefly the opening of the heavens, and the beautiful vision, visible to the eyes of faith, of all the angels and saints praising God. Invite them to think about what this is like, the songs they can hear and the images they can see. Hold this vision with the children, then all say or sing the *Holy, holy, holy* together.

At home

No adaptation is required to do this prayer exercise at home but it would be good to remind the children of this prayer before going to Mass. When at Mass – and at the appropriate time in the Liturgy – children can look upwards and repeat the exercise.

Adapting the traditional Rosary (Mary; Feast Days)

Many traditional forms of prayer and devotion in the Church date back to a time when very few people could read and write. The focus in these prayers is often on repeating familiar prayers, using pictures, creating a prayerful environment in which people feel close to God. The Rosary is one of the greatest forms of praye r– not only allowing a person or group to reach out to God, not only encouraging devotion to Our Lady, but also inviting the person praying to reflect more deeply on the mysteries of faith.

It is easy to adapt the Rosary for children. The teacher may introduce the children to the idea of praying with beads (if they are not already familiar). The teacher then continues to outline the traditional way of praying the beads (one Our Father, ten Hail Marys, one Glory be). The teacher may then introduce a simple way of praying the beads for classroom or home use.

Pray

The traditional 'Mysteries' are followed, but only one Hail Mary is prayed for each mystery. For example, on the first bead of the first decade, the mystery is announced and explained by the teacher: *The Annunciation – when the Angel Gabriel told Mary she was to give birth to Jesus, God's Son* (one Hail Mary is said). Then on the second bead, the next mystery is announced: *The Visitation – when Mary shared her joyful news with Elizabeth* (one Hail Mary is said). This continues for as many of the Mysteries as there is time for. Perhaps the Joyful Mysteries are enough for one session, the Sorrowful for the next session and so on.

Finger Prayer (General)

Some types of creative prayer require resources to be available: others use simply what is available all the time. Finger Prayer recalls the way most children have learned to count – on their fingers. This way of praying needs only the person offering the prayer, and their hand (or hands!)

Pray

Beginning with the left hand, invite the children to hold up one finger. Looking at that finger, they think of someone or something they want to pray for, and they speak to God in their heart about that intention, explaining why they are praying to God for it. Then they hold up a second finger, and pray an intention (a person or thing) for that finger. They can continue for the whole hand.

On the other hand, they then hold up one finger, and name something they want to thank God for. They explain silently to God what it is, and why they are grateful to God; and so on for the rest of the hand. The prayer session can conclude with the children each (silently) praying a Hail Mary.

At home

Children can return to the prayer later on in the day and see if they can remember the intentions on each finger of each hand, and make the prayer again.

Lego Bridge (Sorrow; Renewal of life)

Prayer is always a movement, from us to God, and from God to us. Sometimes we pray for change, that God will help us, or help someone else, by changing them or us. We want some kind of transformation, and want God to make it happen for us. A good image for this kind of prayer is that of a bridge: we begin on one side, cross over whatever is holding us back or preventing the change, and we end up on the other side.

Pray

Explain to the children that in this prayer they will be crossing a bridge. They write on one half of a piece of paper how things are now, and on the other half how they wish God to make things. Then they build a simple, single-span Lego bridge, and imagine in prayer crossing from one side to the other: from how things are, to how they want God to make them. One bridge may suffice for a whole class, it being passed round during the prayer to bridge each individual prayer paper; or if there are sufficient Lego resources, each child may build their own bridge. Older children may be encouraged to illustrate their thought pictorially.

Bring the prayer to a conclusion with the Our Father.

At home

No adaptation is required to do this prayer exercise at home.

Stations of the Cross (General)

Found in every Catholic Church, the Stations of the Cross are a way of using the imagination in prayer. Dating from the Middle Ages, when it was the life ambition of many Catholics to go on pilgrimage to the Holy Land, but an ambition impossible for most to fulfil, the Stations enabled a 'pilgrimage of the heart', a way of being in spirit with Jesus on his last journey. Although not one of the traditional fourteen Stations, the Resurrection is important as it is an essential part of the story, and it will help children to see beyond the suffering and death of Jesus.

Pray

The Stations of the Cross can easily be adapted for children, not just for communal celebration, but also for personal prayer. Children may be invited to draw their own Stations (a reduced number of Stations is helpful here: for example, Jesus is unjustly condemned; Jesus is crowned with thorns; Jesus receives his cross; Jesus falls; Jesus meets his mother; Simon helps Jesus; Jesus is crucified; Jesus is placed in the tomb; Jesus rises again). Stations are numbered and placed around the classroom or hall and each has a title explaining what it is. The children are invited to slowly walk around the classroom or hall, stopping at each station for a short while. The short prayer 'Thank you Jesus' (or something else appropriate and perhaps created by the children) is recited privately by each child at each Station.

A variation of this is for the teacher to project each Station in turn (perhaps three a day) for a minute at a time, with the children repeating to themselves the suggested prayer, as they contemplate the individual Stations.

At home

No adaptation is required to do this prayer exercise at home.

God's wardrobe (Holy Spirit)

In his letter to the Colossians, Saint Paul urges his fellow Christians to possess patience, kindness, and above all, love. The believer is to dress him or herself in every virtue, and love will hold all the virtues together. This concept uses a notion familiar to children, and can prove a fruitful experience of prayer.

Pray

Invite the children to name virtues that are good to have, prompting them where necessary. Display a list of these virtues where they can be clearly seen. Describe this list as God's wardrobe, and explain that the children are going to dress themselves from this wardrobe.

The children pray to themselves, 'From God's wardrobe I am putting on …' and here they name a virtue, saying why they are putting it on. For example, 'From God's wardrobe I am putting on patience, because it will help me not to answer back at home'. Then they will choose another virtue, and repeat the process. After time has been given for several 'garments' to be selected, the Glory be to the Father can be said together, thanking God for all that is in the wardrobe, to be worn by us all.

When this exercise is repeated during the week, additional virtues can be chosen by the children and added as 'garments'.

At home

No adaptation is required to do this prayer exercise at home; however, family members could all participate to make this more of a family prayer experience rather than one that is individual.

Hand-washing for Sorrow (Sorrow)

Washing ourselves is a routine part of life. We keep ourselves clean so that we look clean, so that we smell clean – and cleanliness is vital for hygiene. We're also familiar with the expression, 'Cleanliness is next to Godliness' – this is linking our physical clean-ness with our moral purity. In one of the Psalms, the repentant sinner asks, 'Wash away all my sin, and cleanse me from all my guilt'. In this prayer exercise, we are continuing this theme of washing and asking God's forgiveness.

Pray

The teacher introduces the prayer exercise by talking about the importance of everyday cleanliness; then about how sin is something that spoils our cleanliness before God; about how God washes away our sin when we ask for forgiveness. The children are invited to pray in their own heart for God's forgiveness for anything they might have done wrong.

Each child is invited to come forward to a bowl of warm water and say silently, *'Dear God, please wash away all my sins, and make me clean'*. The children wash their hands, dry them, and return to their place. A sign of the cross can end this prayer exercise.

(Children who are old enough to receive the sacrament of reconciliation should be reminded of the wonder and beauty of this sacrament and be encouraged to receive it on a regular basis.)

Breath of the Spirit (Holy Spirit)

There is no description of the Holy Spirit anywhere in the Old or New Testaments of the Bible, but the Spirit of God is often compared to something (a dove, tongues of flame, a rushing wind, a gentle breeze). All of these are images of movement and energy. In this prayer exercise, children will focus on the Spirit as a wind, as something whose effects can be seen and felt.

Pray

Each child will be provided with coloured pencils, a square of paper, and a drawing pin. Talk the children through the Gifts of the Holy Spirit, listing them *(Wisdom, Understanding, Courage, Knowledge, Reverence, Right Judgement, Wonder and Awe)*. Invite the children to decorate the paper by writing and colouring the different Gifts. Fold the papers into windmills, and pin each windmill to a pencil (see http://www.faa.gov/education_research/education/student_resources/kids_corner/ages_5_9/make_a_windmill/ for instructions).

Each child then prays silently for a few moments, 'Please, Lord, give me the Gifts of the Holy Spirit', and then blows on the windmill. This exercise is repeated seven times. A prayer may be said together to close the exercise.

For younger children, replace the gifts written on the windmills with pictures of the effects of the Holy Spirit. When blowing the windmill the children pray silently, 'Holy Spirit make me strong'.

Feather Prayer (Holy Spirit)

One of the medieval saints of the Church, Abbess Hildegard, compared herself to 'a feather on the breath of God'. God was the great king, she said, who stooped down from his throne, picked up a tiny feather, and then blew it this way and that. In the same way, she said, did God have control of her life. Here, we have breath and feather (dove), two images of the Spirit of God.

Pray

Introduce this idea to the children. Give each child a small feather (such as those found in a feather pillow), or invite them to tear their own feather from a piece of thin tissue. Tell them that the feather represents themselves. Ask the children to stand up, carefully drop the feather and gently blow it, watching where it goes. As they do this, ask them to remember that the Spirit guides their lives. The exercise may be repeated several times in one session. To end the session, invite the children to pray, 'Come Holy Spirit' three times.

At home

No adaptation is required to do this prayer exercise at home.

Praying the Saints (Saints; Guidance)

Saints, in our Catholic tradition, are our friends, examples, guides, encouragers, heavenly neighbours – those who have gone before us and now live fully in the presence of God. God's concerns are their concerns, so they help us with their prayers. We celebrate their individual feasts, we invoke them during every Mass, we celebrate All Saints.

Pray

Provide the children with a picture or icon of the saint/saints to be celebrated. Describe their life, where possible. List their virtues – traits that are good. Ask the children to draw and colour a picture based on the picture before them. Around the drawing, invite them to write the virtues of the saint. When the drawing is complete, invite each child to look at their drawing in silence. Ask them to enter into conversation with the saint (who is in heaven, before God), and to say, 'Saint John (for example), pray for me to God so I will be like you in courage', and to repeat this prayer, each time inserting a different virtue. The prayer may be adapted, the child saying, for example, 'Saint *John*, pray for my family, Saint *John*, pray for those who are sick, Saint *John*, pray for my friends …'

End the exercise with a prayer to Our Lady.

On the Telephone (Coping with life)

Most people in our country today, young and old, use the telephone – at home, on the street, at work, wherever. It's a quick and convenient way of keeping in touch. It is essentially informal, conversational, sometimes planned, often spontaneous. It's a part of life. We don't think twice about giving someone a ring over matters trivial or important. The ease with which we can speak over the telephone, and the connected-ness we're used to, are pointers to children in personal prayer. God is always available for a chat; God always looks forward to hearing from us; we don't have to stand on formality with God; frequent chats keep our relationship with God fresh.

Pray

Invite the children to close their eyes, and to hold an imaginary telephone to their ear. Let them imagine telephoning God. God answers on the first ring, and is delighted to receive the call. Let them imagine the conversation that follows, where they share the joys, concerns and sorrows of life, imagining God's peaceful, patient, kind, gentle, loving response. Bring the conversations to an end with a Glory be to the Father.

This prayer experience can be even more effective if the children are able to speak aloud when engaging in conversation with God, as they would do when telephoning someone in normal circumstances. However, their conversations with and their prayer to God are personal, so, where possible, children should be positioned appropriately to allow for maximum privacy.

At home

This prayer activity would work well at home, in the comfort and privacy of the child's own room or space.

Prayer of Life (Praise; Faithful Departed)

The proper context for all prayer is remembering that we owe everything to God, we are nothing without God, that God is the Creator of all. When we keep this in mind, we can give thanks, ask for all that we need, and give praise. This prayer is thanksgiving and praise for the gift of life: for our life, for all life. It may be prayed seasonally, for example in Spring, or at any time of the year.

Pray

Ask the children to bring something living into school – a leaf, a flower, a seed or a bud (animals are not recommended here!). Introduce the whole notion of life as God's gift to us, life as something which depends on God to sustain it, and eternal life as God's promise to those who love God. Invite the children to think of as many living things and people as they can (allow two or three minutes for this). Invite children to repeat silently, over and over again, 'Let everything that lives, give praise to God'. After a couple of minutes, change the refrain to 'Let all people sing the praise of God'. Finally, change the refrain to 'Let all the saints in heaven rejoice in God's love'. Finish with the Our Father.

Mirror Prayer (Self-affirmation; Service)

The Book of Genesis tells us we are made in the image and likeness of God. Sometimes this is hard to believe of ourselves and of others. God's image in us can be obscured, and this prayer exercise helps to remind us of who made us, in whose image we are made, and that we are made to love. The command of Jesus is to 'Love your neighbour as you love yourself' – both parts of the command are necessary.

Pray

Provide each child with a mirror (e.g. one large mirror for all, a mirror each, a spoon each, where the child can see their reflection). Invite the children to study their own reflection for a minute, noting all the details. Then invite them to say silently over and over, 'This is the person God loves'. After a couple of minutes, change the refrain to 'This is the person who loves God'. Then finally, change the refrain to 'This is the person who loves other people'. Finish with a Hail Mary.

At home

No adaptation is required to do this prayer exercise at home.

Sweetness Prayer (General; Praise)

The Psalms invite us to 'Taste and see that the Lord is good'. This is a profound invitation. God is not just someone 'out there', distant, untouchable. God is not just someone towards whom we send our prayers, hoping they can cover the vast distance between us and heaven. God comes close. In this prayer, we taste something sweet, and it reminds us of God's goodness.

Pray

Ask the children to bring something sweet to class, a piece of fruit, some juice, a sweet. Speak to them of God's goodness, and about how God comes close to us. Remind them how Jesus gives himself in Holy Communion, and as we eat food for our body, we also need food for our soul.

Invite them to eat (or drink), and as they do so, ask them to think of God's goodness and how God comes close to us. Then invite the children, in the silence of their heart, to say over and over again, 'Taste and see that God is good'.

The Key to Heaven (Faithful Departed; Hope)

On the Cross, Jesus opened his arms to embrace the whole of humanity. By dying and rising again, he opened the gates of Paradise which had been closed by the disobedience of Adam and Eve. People were exiled from their heavenly home, with no hope of eternal life with God. This prayer exercise focuses on the Cross as the key to heaven, the sign by which we, and those whom we love, are admitted to eternal happiness and peace.

Pray

Each child is to make a cross, out of paper, card, sticks, straws – whatever is to hand. The story of Adam and Eve's disobedience and banishment from Paradise is told, and how all was put right by the perfect, loving obedience of Jesus. The Cross of Jesus is the key to heaven. Invite the children to think about this and to say to themselves the names of all those they love and whom they would like to see in Heaven. The key is given to everyone who believes. The death and resurrection of Jesus is the way to everlasting happiness. Invite the children to remember all those who have died, whom Jesus has now welcomed into heaven.

Hands Open (Asking; Thanking)

The universal sign of asking for something is to hold out our open hands, hoping that what we need will be given to us. This is something we all do every day without even thinking about it. It is a most appropriate gesture for prayer, where it is a sign of our need of God, our dependence on God, and our expectation that God will hear us and be generous to us.

Pray

Invite the children to place their hands in their laps, open to receive. Tell them of God's generosity and love. Tell them how Jesus fed people, forgave people, taught people, healed people and loved people. Ask them to close their eyes and to ask God for whatever they need; and then to imagine God gently placing all good things into their open hands. Finish, with hands still open, with the Our Father.

At home

No adaptation is required to do this prayer exercise at home.

One-Minute Prayer (Prayer Anywhere)

Prayer isn't just a series of spiritual exercises that we have to do to please God. And it's not simply conversation with God. It's a whole orientation of life, a whole direction of self towards the God who made us and loves us. So prayer isn't necessarily better because it's longer, or because we feel holy, or because someone's watching. A short, sincere, hidden prayer can be as good as any other kind. God sees all. God reads the heart. This prayer is deliberately short to show that this is true. Explain this to the children. This is a prayer for any place and any time.

Pray

Have a clock with a visible second hand. Tell the children that they will be praying for one minute only. Invite them to pray for as many things and people as they can in that one minute. Tell them when to start. Finish with the Glory be to the Father.

Vary this prayer, suggesting one minute praying for one person, or one minute saying 'Thank you' to God, and so on.

At home

No adaptation is required to do this prayer exercise at home.

Tongues of Flame (Holy Spirit)

The Holy Spirit, Saint John's Gospel tells us, blows freely wherever it wills; the Spirit is alive, dynamic, brings change and brings growth. Like the flame which did not consume the bush burning in the desert, the Spirit hovering over the heads of the disciples at Pentecost did not harm them, but inspired them, giving them courage, new strength, new languages in which to praise God. This prayer exercise recalls those tongues of flame.

Pray

Children are reminded of the coming of God's Spirit, with all the gifts the Spirit brings. They can then be invited to paint with glass paint (as used in crafts, making stained glass). They are to paint their own image or name, above which is fire or a tongue of flame, onto transparent plastic (e.g. OHP transparencies). The resulting transparencies are stuck to a window, or placed with a light shining through them, or put on an OHP. Looking at the image of person and flame, they pray repeatedly in silence, 'Come, Holy Spirit, fill us with your love', or, 'Holy Spirit of God, come down on us, come down on your Church'. End by saying, or preferably singing, 'Veni Sancte Spiritus' (Taizé).

Mother Mary (Mary)

From his Cross, Jesus said to John, 'Son, behold your mother', and then to Mary, 'Woman, behold your son'. Mary as mother was given to the Church; she is our mother, and the mother of all who believe. She cares for each of us in a special way. If we are like Mary, we will care for other people.

Pray

Set up a classroom crib. Instead of the child Jesus, place a basket or other suitably sized container. Explain to each child that Mary and Joseph watched over the baby Jesus. In this prayer, we are asking them to watch over the people we commend to their care. We are going to write down a name (or names) and place them in the basket in the crib. But not only are Mary and Joseph going to watch over them: we are going to pray for them each day for one week! Once the names are placed in the crib, invite the children to pray silently for their name. This should be repeated each day during the week.

Hot-water bottle Prayer (God's Love)

God is all-powerful, all-knowing, and beyond our understanding. But at the same time, God is a loving God, cares infinitely for us, and is always inviting us to come closer. Prayer is one of the ways in which we come closer to God. It is sometimes hard though to approach God, when we can hardly imagine what God is like. This exercise is using one of the senses, touch, and the idea of warmth to help us to think of the warmth of God's love for each of us.

Pray

All that is needed for the prayer session is a covered hot-water bottle, filled with hot (but not too hot) water. The gospel passage about the little children (Luke 18:15-17) is read to children, along with the explanation that Jesus wanted the children near him because he loved them: a gentle, warm, accepting love. As the hot-water bottle is passed round, invite each child to hold it for a few moments, to feel the warmth, and to think of the warmth of God's love for them personally. When the bottle is passed on, the warmth remains in their hands. A song or chant may be sung while the bottle is passed round. The session ends with open hands and an 'Our Father' together.

Fizzy-drink Prayer (Holy Spirit; Confirmation)

The Holy Spirit is invisible, but the power of the Holy Spirit is seen in its effect on people's lives: an effect that can be dramatic as well as quiet and peaceful. The Holy Spirit inspires people who normally would be shy to share their faith boldly; those who would be confused to understand; those who would be lost to see their way; and those who would be quiet and undemonstrative to live their faith openly. This exercise is a dramatic demonstration of hidden power – which must be performed outside, with supervision!

All that's needed is an explanation of the unseen way in which the Spirit comes to people, and the effects the Spirit can have in a person's life. Explain to the children that this prayer will be quick (and too messy to be tried at home!).

Pray

Take a large, unopened plastic bottle of fizzy drink (1 litre or more of Coke, lemonade etc.). After the explanation above has been given, open the bottle and drop in several sugary sweets (eg. Refreshers, Mentos) and then stand well back. The fizzy drink will erupt in a fountain from the bottle. While this takes place, ask the children to shout, 'Holy Spirit, change my life!' again and again, louder and louder.

Breathing Prayer (Life; Spirit; Prayer)

God breathes out, and God's breath gives life. But God's breath is not some kind of magical mist, but an expression of God's very self. This breath is the Holy Spirit, the spirit of life. One part of the Holy Trinity, one of the three persons of the One God. We can't understand this, and we can't describe it adequately. But we know what breathing is, how necessary it is to life, how much we take it for granted each and every moment of our lives. In this prayer, our breathing reminds us of God's Spirit, and of the Spirit's role in our lives.

Pray

Explain to the children the importance of breath, and the necessity of breath for life. We can breathe in only because we have already breathed out, and vice-versa. Our first independent act after birth is an intake of breath; and our last breath is breathing out. Invite the children to be still, and to be aware of their own breathing. Suggest that with an outward breath, they breathe out something negative or unwholesome, and with an intake of breath they take in goodness. Allow a few seconds' break, and repeat the pattern. For example, breathe out fear, breathe in courage; breathe out resentment, breathe in forgiveness; breathe out rejection, breathe in acceptance. (For younger children, only one negative and one positive thing should be repeated as they breathe in and out.) Continue the exercise for two or three minutes (perhaps shorter for younger children). Finish with 'Glory be to the Father'.

At home

No adaptation is required to do this prayer exercise at home.

My name for the day (General)

We are all known by our names: our first name, by which we are called every day by family, friends, teachers and others. And we have our family name that suggests who we belong to, where we are from. These family names often originated in the occupations, national origins or clan/family associations of our ancestors. But we can be known by other names too: nicknames or even initials. In this exercise, each child will take a new, secret name for the day, and try to live up to that name. No-one else will know what that name is. They might be able to guess, but that is not the main point of this exercise.

Pray

After explaining this, the teacher prepares slips of paper, each with a 'name' on it, with a brief explanation, and a couple of suggestions about how this name might be lived up to. The children can be involved in the preparation of these slips. Examples would be: **Name**: Kindness; **Meaning**: Doing good things for other people; **Suggestions**: Let someone else go first; say something nice to someone.

Each child picks out a slip of paper, and keeps it with them for the day, attempting to live what it describes. At the end of the day the slips may be returned to be used again another day.

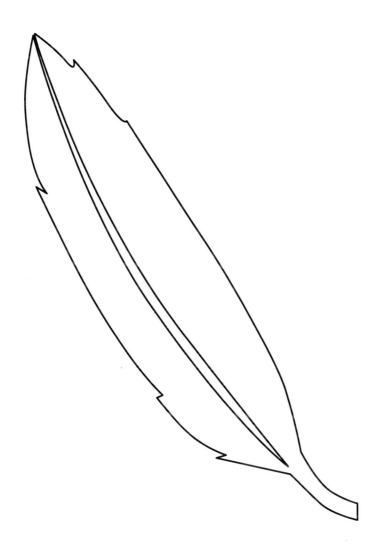

Praying with Gabriel
Feather template
(Not to scale)

Praying with Gabriel
Angel template
(Not to scale)